SUPPORTING STUDENTS WITH LEARNING NEEDS IN THE BLOCK

Marcia Conti-D'Antonio

Robert Bertrando

and

Joanne Eisenberger

EYE ON EDUCATION

EYE ON EDUCATION
6 DEPOT WAY WEST, SUITE 106
LARCHMONT, NY 10538
(914) 833–0551
(914) 833–0761 fax

Library of Congress Cataloging-in-Publication Data

Conti-D'Antonio, Marcia, 1953–
    Supporting students with learning needs in the block / by Marcia Conti-D'Antonio, Robert Bertrando, Joanne Eisenberger.
        p.   cm.— (Teaching in the block)
    Includes bibliographical references (p.   ).
    ISBN 1-883001-54-4
    1. Schedules, School—United States. 2. Inclusive education—United States. I. Bertrando, Robert, 1941–. II. Eisenberger, Joanne, 1042–. III. Title. IV. Series.
    LB3032.C66   1998
    371.2'42—dc21   97-51879
                                                                                                                    CIP

10 9 8 7 6 5 4 3 2

Editorial and production services provided by Richard H. Adin Freelance Editorial Services, 9 Orchard Drive, Gardiner, NY 12525 (914-883-5884)

Other Books on Block Scheduling

Teaching in the Block
Stategies for Engaging Active Learners
edited by Robert Lynn Canady and Michael D. Rettig

Block Scheduling
A Catalyst For Change in High Schools
by Robert Lynn Canady and Michael D. Rettig

Middle School Block Scheduling
by Robert Lynn Canady and Michael D. Rettig

The 4 X 4 Block Schedule
by J. Allen Queen and Kimberly Gaskey Isenhour

Action Research On Block Scheduling
by David Marshak

Teaching in the Block, the series
Robert Lynn Canady and Michael D. Rettig, General Editors

Supporting Students With Learning Needs in the Block
by Marcia Conti-D'Antonio, Robert Bertrando, and Joanne Eisenberger

Teaching Mathematics in the Block
by Susan Gilkey and Carla Hunt

Teaching Foreign Languages in the Block
by Deborah Blaz

For more information on Teaching in the Block, contact us at:

Eye On Education
6 Depot Way West
Larchmont, NY 10538
phone (914) 833-0551
fax (914) 833-0761
www.eyeoneducation.com

Also Published by Eye On Education

Performance Assessment and Standards-Based Curricula
The Achievement Cycle
by Allan A. Glatthorn

The Performance Assessment Handbook
Volume 1: Portfolios and Socratic Seminars
Volume 2: Performances and Exhibitions
by Bil Johnson

A Collection of Performance Tasks and Rubrics

Middle School Mathematics
by Charlotte Danielson

Upper Elementary School Mathematics
by Charlotte Danielson

High School Mathematics
by Charlotte Danielson and Elizabeth Marquez

The School Portfolio
A Comprehensive Framework for School Improvement
by Victoria L. Bernhardt

Research on Educational Innovations, 2d ed.
by Arthur K. Ellis and Jeffrey T. Fouts

School-to-Work
by Arnold H. Packer and Marion W. Pines

The Reflective Supervisor
A Practical Guide for Educators
by Ray Calabrese and Sally Zepeda

Instruction and the Learning Environment
by James Keefe and John Jenkins

The Educator's Brief Guide to the Internet and the World Wide Web
by Eugene F. Provenzo

DEDICATION

We dedicate this book to our parents Frank and Antoinette Conti, Arthur and Hazel Shull, and William and Catherine Bertrando, and to the Bertrando boys, Chris, Marc, and Michael, and to all the other teachers and students who have shaped and continue to shape our lives.

FOREWORD

Block schedules provide opportunities for teachers to change their instructional strategies so that students become more active and successful learners. There is a growing body of evidence from experiences with high school block scheduling that strongly supports the notion that with proper staff development and careful schedule design the overall school environment becomes more positive and productive. There is also evidence that many teachers increase their personal contacts with students. Furthermore, when curricular and instructional issues are addressed appropriately, achievement in many schools improves, as measured by factors such as reduced failure rates, increased number of students on honor rolls, and higher test scores.

Because we believe that instructional change is the key to successful block scheduling, we are sponsoring this series of books, written primarily by teachers who have been successful in teaching in block schedules. While we believe this series can be helpful to teachers working in any type of schedule, the ideas should be especially useful for middle and high school teachers who are "Teaching in the Block."

The idea of scheduling middle and high schools in some way other than daily, single periods is not new. We find in educational history numerous attempts to modify traditional schedules and to give the instructional school day greater flexibility. In the 1960s, for example, approximately 15% of American high schools implemented modular scheduling, which typically combined "mods" of time to create schedules with instructional periods that varied in length from between 15 minutes to classes of 100 minutes or more.

Many reasons have been given for the demise of modular scheduling as practiced during the 1960s and 1970s. However, two of the primary reasons often cited are that (1) too much independent study time was included in those schedules and school management became a problem, and (2) teachers in many schools did not receive training designed to assist them in altering instruction in the longer class period (Canady and Rettig, 1995, pp. 13–15). Current models of block scheduling do not include significant built-in independent study time and, therefore, school management problems are not exacerbated, but helped. We have found, however, that in schools where block scheduling has been implemented successfully, considerable attention has been paid to adapting instruction to maximize the potential of available time.

We repeatedly have stated that if schools merely "change their bells," block scheduling should not be implemented. We also have contended that if teachers are not provided with extensive staff development, block scheduling will be a problem. "The success or failure of the [current] block scheduling movement will be determined largely by the ability of teachers...to improve instruction. Regardless of a school's time schedule, what happens between individual teachers and students in classrooms is still most important, and simply altering the manner in which we schedule school will not ensure better instruction by teachers or increased learning by students" (Canady & Rettig, 1995, p. 240).

In this book, Marcia Conti-D'Antonio, Robert Bertrando, and Joanne Eisenberger demonstrate that block schedules provide opportunities for educators to address the needs of diverse populations of students. The inclusion of learning disabled, physically disabled, and gifted and talented students into regular classrooms provides new challenges for educators. Middle school and high school content teachers may meet with students whose dominant language is not English. Some students may have been identified as being "at-risk"; others may have been identified as having an attention deficit disorder (ADD). Block scheduling provides extended time for these (and all) students to process information in a connected curriculum rather than during fragmented periods of study.

In the first part of this book, the authors offer details for both content teachers and support teachers about how inclusion can work in a block-scheduled school. In the appendices, the authors provide examples of checklists, model forms, and student handouts that teachers can use to provide support for students with learning needs. These appendices will appeal to educators in all schools, including those that have not implemented an inclusion model.

Robert Lynn Canady
Michael D. Rettig

Please share with us…

Eye On Education is interested in learning about your experiences teaching in the block. Please let us know about:

a lesson plan that worked especially well

♦ a strategy that harnessed the potential of the extended period

♦ an anecdote that shows how block scheduling influenced the learning process

Please write, phone, or e-mail us at:

Eye On Education
6 Depot Way West
Larchmont, NY 10538
(914) 833-0551 phone
(914) 833-0761 fax
block@eyeoneducation.com

PREFACE

Our intentions in writing *Supporting Students with Learning Needs in the Block* were threefold. First, we wanted to show that school districts can successfully meet the challenges of inclusion in a block schedule. Second, we wanted to offer specific information on how the content teachers and support teachers can share the responsibilities inclusion demands. We offer specific advice on how cooperative planning and teaching will give students with learning needs the best opportunity to experience success. Third, we wanted to place in the hands of teachers specific, practical teaching suggestions that will increase student achievement.

This volume is a treasure trove of tried and true strategies that enhance learning for students with learning needs and for regular education students. Administrators who must meet the challenges of inclusion will find this book to be invaluable as they develop block schedules that support students with learning needs. Support teachers will refer to this book as they plan and teach cooperatively with content teachers. Content teachers, faced with meeting the challenges of restructuring and inclusion, will rely on this book to choose researched-based best practices. This book will be a reference on the desks of all reflective educators who believe that:

- all students can achieve
- restructuring offers new and exciting opportunities
- varying instructional methodology promotes learning
- differentiating instruction allows all students to be successful
- cooperative planning and teaching enhances the delivery of instruction
- heterogeneity provides unique learning possibilities for all students

ABOUT THE AUTHORS

Marcia Conti-D'Antonio is currently training and providing technical assistance to new teachers in the Unionville-Chadds Ford School District. She has been in public education for 23 years with teaching experiences in elementary education, special education K-12, as well as experience in diagnosis of learning-disabled students. She directed two federally funded projects to train educators to teach special education students included in their classrooms. She earned her masters degree in special education from Temple University and completed her graduate work in reading at the University of Pennsylvania.

Joanne Eisenberger has been in public education for 36 years. After two years in the Peace Corps in Liberia, she taught mainstreamed special education classes in Washington, California, New York, and Pennsylvania. She is currently teaching high school and middle school classes that provide support primarily for students with Attention Deficit Disorder in the Unionville-Chadds Ford School District. She earned her masters degree in special education from San Francisco University.

Robert Bertrando is the social studies supervisor for the Unionville Chadds-Ford School District. He has been in the field of public education for 35 years, having begun his teaching career as an English/social studies teacher. He has been involved in designing and coordinating district initiatives to adapt curriculum and instruction to meet the needs of the diversified learner. He earned his B.A. from The Pennsylvania State University and his masters degree from West Chester University.

TABLE OF CONTENTS

ACKNOWLEDGEMENTS

We'd like to recognize these fellow teachers who kept us honest by providing some of the practical feedback to our chapters: Robert Conti-D'Antonio, Unionville-Chadds Ford School District; Mary Ann Frabriso-Maloney, Avon Grove School District; and Fern Aefsky, Monroe-Woodbury Central School District. We'd like to thank both Robert Lynn Canady and Michael Rettig for their supportive faxes, phone calls, and letters. Publisher Robert Sickles provided guidance during this, our first, effort. Finally, we must acknowledge our spouses, Rob, Sandy, and Bob for their humor and patience.

1

INTRODUCTION

THE CHALLENGES OF INCLUSION AND BLOCK SCHEDULING

The issues related to educating a diverse population of students reflect the growing heterogeneity of students in classrooms across the United States. This book assists school personnel who must deal with the realities of new national content standards and the push for inclusion of all students in content classrooms, as well as the anticipated demands of the 21st century.

National content standards have set the stage for how students must be prepared for the 21st century. Students will need to learn how to live and be productive within an increasingly diverse population. They also must find their place in a society that uses technology to access massive amounts of information.

In addition, because of the national Individual with Disabilities Education Act (IDEA), reauthorized in the summer of 1997, content teachers are faced with the inclusion of students who would previously have been educated in a segregated setting. Gifted and talented, learning disabled, mentally disabled, physically disabled, and severely impaired students are to be "educated to the maximum extent appropriate…with children who are not handicapped" (PL 94-142, § 1412). Middle school and high school content teachers also may have students whose dominant language is not English, or whose reading ability is so low that they may receive additional Chapter 1 supportive instruction. Some students may be identified as having an attention deficit disorder (ADD). Also, teachers may have academically talented students in their content classes for whom enrichment will be expected.

Lastly, because school restructuring is commonplace, teachers at the local level are required to rethink student achievement and how best to increase it. The challenge is to see the interconnectedness of these initiatives and to respond to those changes in a way that enhances student learning. Teachers must choose the soundest educational practices and incorporate those habits into daily action. We discuss in this book the research-based best practices when teaching diverse and at-risk learners in a block schedule. But, the strategies and practices are beneficial for all students. The most effective instructional practices for inclusion are often practices that are effective for all students to achieve their greatest potential. Emphasis is placed on maintaining curricula that reflect high standards.

Block scheduling supports these research-based best practices by providing extended time for students to process information in a connected curriculum rather than during fragmented periods of study. Teaching students with diverse learning needs in a block schedule allows for an extended period of consistency, limiting class and teacher changes. Increasing class time allows for more in-depth involvement with curricular concepts. This extended block of time can promote success for the wide variety of students, especially when there are many students who require extended time for processing information (Canady & Rettig, 1996). Administrators and teachers must decide how best to support both the diverse learner and the content teacher who are involved with intensive or block scheduling. A challenge exists if a school district embraces both the initiative of inclusion and of block scheduling. It is much easier to program for students with learning needs in isolation. Guidance and examination of good program models are essential if students with learning needs and their teachers are to be given the support they require to be successful within a block schedule.

PROVIDING A CONTINUUM OF SERVICES

When developing a block schedule that supports inclusive education for all students, a continuum of services must be maintained to meet the needs of a variety of students in a responsible way. In addition, the schedule needs to allow time to meet the unique demands of inclusion. The administrator, guidance counselor, or support teacher should build the students' schedules carefully. The scheduling usually requires a departure from computer-built schedules. After the master schedule has been established, the students who will be supported in content classes must be given priority schedules. This priority guarantees the support teacher access to the students, to cooperative planning periods with content teachers, and liaison meeting times with additional staff and students. The students' schedules should be built first and the support teachers' schedules should be built around them.

Those students who need only monthly or weekly meetings to monitor progress and maintain successful habits can be seen during homeroom or from study halls. Those students who need more strategy instruction than they can receive during a subject area block need to be scheduled for either short-term supportive instruction or for specific instructional periods with a support teacher. Opportunities for both short-term and long-term support curriculum should be planned into the students' and teachers' schedules. Educators must also plan for those students who, to be successful, need supplanted education in self-contained classes. To meet these varying needs, the support teacher's schedule needs to balance time with content teachers, to plan and teach collaboratively, with time to see students with learning needs for direct instruction. Because some content teachers will have students with learning needs but will not be scheduled for collaborative teaching, additional time for miniplanning and informational meetings also must be planned into the schedules. These teacher liaison meetings have multiple purposes which include monitoring the progress of the more successful students, planning for the implementation of student accommodations, and answering content teacher concerns.

SCHEDULES THAT SUPPORT STUDENTS WITH LEARNING NEEDS

In any block schedule format, content education teachers and support teachers can share the responsibilities of teaching, planning, monitoring, and assessing student progress. It is also possible for any student to reach a support teacher in a variety ways. Some students will need feedback and quick conferences about their progress in their courses. In all the block schedules that follow, we have called this meeting between the support teachers and their students *student liaison*. When students are with the support teacher for a short-term but intensive strategy instruction or adaptive education, the block is called *student liaison and study*. These blocks provide access to instruction for students who may not have a support teacher cooperatively teaching in any of their classes, as well as for those students who need very specific strategy instruction. For long-term support and ongoing instruction in strategies for success, the block is called *learning to learn*. Students are scheduled into the learning to learn blocks for course credit, and a program of instruction for class credit is delivered by the support teacher. This is also the place where the goals and objectives of Individual Education Plan (IEP) are taught. The blocks of sustained, supplanted instruction still needed by some students are called *supplanted instruction* or *special education*. In all the block schedules, it is helpful to schedule the students' elective courses so that these courses can be dropped and replaced with a learning to learn or student liaison and study period for specific strategy instruction. The students' elective class periods can also be positioned to allow for supplanted instruction if such serious intervention becomes necessary.

The support teachers' schedules that follow use the same language as the student schedules. The meetings to gather the information from content teachers to prepare to give the students feedback we call *teacher liaison*. When support teachers are teaching and planning with a content teacher, the blocks are called *co-teaching* and *co-planning*. These blocks are planned into the support teachers' schedules: when large numbers of students with learning needs have enrolled in a particular course; when a student who is very limited is enrolled in a course; or when a content teacher has requested a support teacher for assistance in learning how to provide the students with their accommodations without watering down the curriculum.

THE 4/4 SEMESTER PLAN

In the 4/4 semester plan (Figure 1.1), students take four courses a semester. In a 7-hour school day, these courses meet for approximately 90 minutes each day. Teachers work with only three groups of students daily and most of the traditional year-long courses are completed in a single semester. This plan allows students with learning needs appropriate periods with support teachers and full inclusion into regular education classes. The 4/4 model in Figure 1.1 is built on the premise that a program aimed at producing independent students requires a great deal of attention to courses and pupils at the 9th and 10th grade level. If these 9th and 10th grade students can acquire and internalize the strategies for test taking (see Appendices F and L for test taking), composing, self-advocacy and self-determination (see Appendix H for self-advocacy and self-determination), time and materials management, and comprehension (see Appendix I for constructing for knowledge), less supportive service will be required during subsequent school years. To maintain a continuum of service, blocks of time are planned into the second semester for supplanted instruction. These blocks can be used for a student who needs to make up a failed course through a support teacher's class. This supplanted instruction should be a very unusual occurrence if the appropriate supportive services for content teachers and the appropriate accommodations for special needs students are in place.

In some cases, a high school may need to provide a support program that is more self-contained and must provide much more supplanted instruction. Content subjects can be taught in a special education block when the needs of the special education students limit inclusion. In this type of student's schedule, the time frame would be most similar to the 9th grade schedule shown is Figure 1.7 (p. 17).

The schedule shown in Figure 1.1 is that of four students with learning disabilities or attention deficit disorders. The 9th grader begins his day in English class. This class has two teachers—a content expert English teacher and a support teacher. When he leaves English class he has an elective course such as art or music. Following the elective, he reports to a support teacher's class called learning to learn. There he learns and practices the strategies he will need to memorize information (see Appendix G for memorizing), identify key information, request accommodations, sustain his attention (see Appendix E for sustaining attention), and organize his materials (see Appendix K for organizing time and materials). If his learning needs have been met by this instruction, he will proceed to lunch and another elective for part of the first semester. If he needs more instruction, this elective will be dropped and he will report to class with a support teacher for a liaison (feedback from his content area teachers) and study period. He will end the day in a western civilization class which also has two teachers, a content teacher and a support teacher.

FIGURE 1.1. 4/4 BLOCK SCHEDULE

High School Special Needs Students Enrolled in Content Classes: 22-Credit Diploma 4/4 Block Schedule using 4 blocks daily; 8 courses annually, 2 lunch/activity periods

Times	9th Grader		10th Grader		11th Grader		12th Grader	
	First Semester							
8:00–9:30	English		Biology I		U.S. History		Integrated English/ Econ. & Govt (2 Credits)	
9:34–11:00	Elective		Geometry		Elective			
11:04–11:30	Learning to Learn		Lunch		Lunch		Liaison and Study	
11:34–12:00	Lunch		Elective	PE	Learning to Learn		Lunch	
12:04–1:30	Elective	Health/ PE	Learning to Learn		Elective		Elective	PE
1:34–3:00	West Civ.		Elective		Algebra II		Work Experience	
	Second Semester							
8:00–9:30	Algebra I		English		English		Elective	
9:34–11:00	Physical Science		Elective		Chem. In Community		Algebra III & Trig.	
11:04–11:30	Lunch		Liaison and Study		Study and Liaison		Lunch	
11:34–12:00	Elective		Lunch		Lunch		Liaison and Study	
12:04–1:30	Elective	Computer	Afro/Asian Studies		Elective	PE	Work Experience	
1:34–3:00	Elective		Elective		Elective			

A 4/4 semester teaching schedule for a support teacher (Figure 1.2) also must be constructed carefully to allow for the demands of inclusion. The support teacher's schedule needs to balance time for content teachers and support teachers to meet, plan, and teach collaboratively (co-teaching and co-planning). Time also must be planned for discussions with content teachers about students' progress in courses that are not being planned or taught collaboratively (teacher liaison). Times for the support teacher to provide direct, intensive, adaptive, or tutorial supplemental strategy instruction (learning to learn) need to be scheduled. Finally, long-term supplanted instruction (special education instruction) must be built into the schedule in the event it is needed. The 4/4 block schedule in Figure 1.2 shows the schedules of three support teachers and assumes that early intervention and intensive instruction aimed at making students independent requires a great deal of attention to courses and students at the 9th and 10th grade levels. The block schedule also assumes that some teachers will have students with learning needs but cannot plan or teach cooperatively with a support teacher. However, 25% of the teaching staff will be free during each segment of the block. Whenever a support teacher has a teacher liaison meeting time in his or her schedule, meetings can be arranged to discuss students' progress, arrange for tutorial sessions, or discuss assignments and tests. These courses are mainly at the 11th and 12th grade levels. If students acquire the strategies for success during the first two years of high school, less supportive service from support teachers should be needed at the higher grade levels. Blocks of time are planned into the second semester for supplanted instruction in the event that students will need to make up failed courses through a support teacher's class.

The 4/4 schedule in Figure 1.2 shows a typical day for three support teachers. The #2 teacher begins her day with a cooperative planning session with the western civilization teacher. They meet to plan units, assessments, and lessons. They discuss their concerns about student progress and plan the agenda for the western civilization block. At about 9:00, she leaves the social studies teacher and meets with other teachers to obtain progress reports on other students with learning needs. Twenty-five percent of the teaching staff will be available during this block and she will have made appointments to meet with at least three other content teachers. Her next period is for preparation. She may plan and prepare materials for her student liaison and study group and her learning to learn class. (See Appendix J for methods of communicating student progress.) She may have had requests for information about a particular student to which she needs to respond. She has lunch and then meets with small groups of students to provide feedback on progress and supervise their study. This is her student liaison and study period. These students tend to be independent but might need tutorial or guided practice. Her next class is learning to learn. These students have greater needs and she provides the strategy instruction that will promote independence and self-reliance. (See adaptive education section of Chapter 5 for strategies for promoting independence.) She ends her teaching day working cooperatively in a 9th grade western civilization class with a social studies teacher.

FIGURE 1.2. HIGH SCHOOL SUPPORT TEACHER 4/4 BLOCK SCHEDULE USING A FULL INCLUSION MODEL

This schedule emphasizes strategy instruction and skill building in 9th and 10th grade courses.

Times	Support Teacher #1	Support Teacher #2	Support Teacher #3
First Semester			
8:00–9:30	Co-teach 9th English	Co-planning & Teacher Liaison	Supplanted Instruction
9:34–11:00	Co-planning & Teacher Liaison	Prep Period	Co-teach Geometry
11:00–11:30	Learning to Learn	Lunch	Lunch
11:30–12:00	Lunch	Student Liaison	Student Liaison
12:04–1:30	Student Liaison & Study	Learning to Learn	Co-planning & Teacher Liaison
1:34–3:00	Prep Period	Co-teach West. Civ.	Prep Period
Second Semester			
8:00–9:30	Prep Period	Co-teach 10th English	Student Liaison & Study
9:34–11:00	Co-teach Physical Science	Learning to Learn	Prep Period
11:04–11:30	Lunch	Student Liaison	Lunch
11:34–12:00	Learning to Learn	Lunch	Student Liaison
12:04–1:30	Co-planning & Teacher Liaison	Co-planning English & Teacher Liaison	Co-teach Afro/Asian Studies
1:34–3:00	Supplanted Instruction	Prep Period	Co-plan & Teacher Liaison

As in any innovative process, concerns may arise. Some of the concerns regarding students' need for supportive services when moving to a 4/4 block scheduling are:

♦ The amount of one-to-one and small group contact between support teacher and special needs students may be reduced;

♦ Careful integration of strategies and higher level thinking into content curriculum can be difficult and time consuming;

♦ To shift a content teacher's focus from concentrating exclusively on *what* to learn to also include *how* to learn can be a slow, evolutionary process;

♦ Skill at working collaboratively during teaching and planning may take time to develop;

♦ A commitment from teachers to work cooperatively to meet the needs of all students may come gradually and only as a result of positive experiences over time;

♦ The construction of engaging units of study that go well beyond simple retention may not be in place.

TRIMESTER PLAN

When using a trimester plan (Figure 1.3), students take 2 or 3 core courses every 60 days. The schedule can be adjusted to include year-long or two-semester courses to provide time for advance placement courses or a performance course such as music. The concerns regarding the trimester plan are similar to those for a 4/4 plan. However, the trimester plan has the added advantage of offering a variety of short-term courses. This advantage makes it an ideal schedule for middle schools and alternative schools that offer a wide variety of subjects and specials to all students. This is an extremely complex schedule to create, but it is an option. Figure 1.3 shows a 6th grade schedule with a support teacher cooperatively teaching in content courses.

The schedule in Figure 1.3 shows a 6th grader with learning needs. During the first semester, he begins his day with a homeroom period. He can use part of this time to meet with his support teacher to organize himself for the day or to get tutorial instruction on difficult homework. (See Appendix K for time and material organization strategies). He can, if he chooses, get the same support from his home room or content area teachers during this time. At 8:35 he goes to his 6th grade English class. He has two teachers—a content teacher and a support teacher. This particular class extends over two semesters. After English, he goes to science, a double-block period to allow him to engage in extensive laboratory experiences without interruption. Science is followed by 30 minutes with the support teachers. Homework is started, goals are set, and skills are strengthened. Lunch, music, and homeroom end his day.

FIGURE 1.3. TRIMESTER SCHEDULE FOR A MIDDLE SCHOOL SPECIAL NEEDS STUDENT

This schedule uses a full inclusion model with extended homeroom and three lunch/activity periods.

Times	First Trimester	Second Trimester	Third Trimester
	6th Grader		
8:00–8:30	Homeroom and Study—students have access to learning support teachers and subject area teachers		
8:35–10:00	English (Co-taught with Support Teacher)		TechEd
10:05–11:30	Science	Math (Co-planned with Support Teachers)	
11:35–12:05		Art	Lunch
12:05–12:35	Resource Room	Lunch	Reading
12:35–1:05	Lunch	Home Ec	PE
1:10–2:40	Music	Geography and Social Studies (Co-planned and Co-taught)	
2:45–3:00	Homeroom and Dismissal		

The schedule shown in Figure 1.4 shows a typical day for a support teacher on a trimester schedule. The support teacher has no homeroom duties so that he is free to see individual children who need instruction or structure in how to organize themselves to begin their day. Pencils are located, papers are filed or retrieved from the crevices of bookbags, questions about difficult homework are answered, and assignment notebooks are dated and labeled. (See Appendix K for time and material organization.) During the first and second trimesters the support teacher cooperatively teaches in a 6th grade English class from 8:35 to 10:00. Following the English class, during the first trimester, he has a preparation period. He may place phone calls to parents, document student progress, or prepare for the 6th grade resource room class he will teach later in the day. He goes to lunch from 11:35 to 12:05 and then meets his 6th grade resource room students. He does the tutorial or adaptive education needed for these students. He may give instruction in locating key information in written materials, in using a test preparation routine, in developing time management skills, or in using memory strategies. (See Appendices F and G, and Chapter 5, adaptive education.) At 12:35 he meets with the 6th grade English teacher to plan lessons and units for the class they cooperatively teach. This meeting does not take the entire block of time. He uses the remaining time, plus the following period, to liaison with other teachers, and to gather information about his students' progress, their tutorial needs, and their upcoming assignments.

FIGURE 1.4. TRIMESTER SCHEDULE FOR A MIDDLE SCHOOL SUPPORT TEACHER—FULL INCLUSION MODEL

This schedule uses a full inclusion model with extended homeroom and three lunch/activity periods.

Times	First Trimester	Second Trimester	Third Trimester
	Support Teacher Schedule		
8:00–8:30	Study — students are seen for organization		
8:35–10:00	6th grade English (Co-taught with Content Teacher)		Prep
10:05–11:30	Prep	Co-planning & Prep	7th grade Resource Room
11:35–12:05	Lunch	Lunch	Lunch
12:05–12:35	6th grade Resource Room	Geo. & Soc. St. Co-planning	Teacher Liaison
12:35–1:05	6th English Planning and Teacher Liaison		Geo. & Soc. St. Co-planning
1:10–2:40	Teacher Liaison	Geography and Social Studies (Co-taught with Content Teacher)	
2:45–3:00	Dismissal		

His schedule changes with each trimester, although some classes overlap the semesters. During the second trimester, his homeroom activities and his cooperative teaching activities remain the same. His lunch, however, now begins at 10:05, followed by a cooperative planning session with the 6th grade math teacher. The support teacher cooperatively taught this course last year and the two teachers have agreed that the cooperative planning time is the most valuable time for them. This meeting will not take the entire period and the support teacher spends part of the period in liaison meetings with other teachers who work with his students. He then meets with the geography/social studies teacher to plan cooperatively the class they teach together later in the day. He continues to liaison and plan with the English teacher, and ends his day cooperatively teaching a geography/social studies course.

During the third trimester his schedule shifts again. He still begins his day with students who need structure to begin school, but the English course has ended and he now has a preparation period in that slot. He also begins to work with a group of 7th graders who have been struggling with schoolwork and who have been identified as needing an additional period of adaptive education or tutorial support. He continues to plan with the 6th grade math teacher, has lunch from 12:05 to 12:35, and cooperatively plans and then teaches with the geography/social studies teacher.

ALTERNATE-DAY (OR ALTERNATE-WEEK) SCHEDULES

When functioning on an alternate-day (week) schedule, students and teachers attend classes every other day or every other week for extended blocks of time. The models shown in Figures 1.5 through 1.8 illustrate an alternate-day or week schedule where teachers and students attend three 90-minute periods on day (week) one and three different 90-minute periods on day (week) two. Time has also been allotted for an extended homeroom in the mornings and a single one-hour period over two lunches. These one-hour periods are used for activities and electives and meet for a single semester.

The schedule shown in Figure 1.5 illustrates a typical school day for a 7th or 8th grader who has very severe learning needs and is on an alternate-day block schedule. The 8th grader begins her day with an extended homeroom period. She can seek out her content area teachers for tutorial lessons, her support teacher for strategy instruction or organization, or remain in her homeroom. Sometimes her support teacher seeks her out and works with her to clarify assignments, establish deadlines and time lines, and to organize lockers or bookbags. (See Appendix K and Chapter 5, adaptive education.) During day 1 she is to be in science class from 8:35 to 10:00. She has two teachers in the room—an 8th grade science teacher and a support teacher. The two teachers planned for her participation in the class and adapted assignments, readings, and activities for her. Her second period is a self-contained, special education math class. She works to improve her skill with a calculator, and her automatism with math facts and math processes. Her goal is to be ready to take a general math course in 9th grade. After math she goes to lunch and then to physical education class or home economics, depending on the time of year. Her last class is another period of instruction with her support teacher called learning to learn. Here she strengthens her basic skills, learns to use the accommodations specified in her

Individual Education Plan (IEP), and the strategies that she needs to be success-ful and independent. (See Appendix K and adaptive education.)

FIGURE 1.5. MIDDLE SCHOOL SPECIAL NEEDS STUDENTS: ALTERNATE-DAY (WEEK) BLOCK SCHEDULE USING A PARTIAL INCLUSION MODEL

Homeroom at beginning and end of the day, 2 lunch/activity periods

Times	7th Grader		Blocks
	Day 1 or Week 1	**Day 2 or Week 2**	
8:00–8:30	Homeroom & Study		**Homeroom**
8:35–10:00	Health/PE	Science	**Block 1**
10:05–11:30	Math	Special Ed. English	**Block 2**
11:35–12:35	Music / Art	Tech Ed / Computers	**Lunch & Activities**
12:40–1:10	Lunch		
1:15–2:40	Social Studies & Geography	Learning to Learn	**Block 3**
2:45–3:00	Homeroom & Dismissal		**Homeroom**

Times	8th Grader		Blocks
	Day 1 or Week 1	**Day 2 or Week 2**	
8:00–8:30	Homeroom & Study	Homeroom & Study	**Homeroom**
8:35–10:00	Science	Social Studies & Geography	**Block 1**
10:05–11:30	Special Ed. Math	Health	**Block 2**
11:35–12:05	Lunch		**Lunch and Activities**
12:10–1:10	Computers/PE / Home Ec	Art / Tech Ed	
1:15–2:40	Learning to Learn	Special Ed. English	**Block 3**
2:45–3:00	Homeroom & Dismissal	Homeroom & Dismissal	**Homeroom**

Day 2 also begins with an extended homeroom and she again has the free-dom to seek tutorial assistance. Her first period class on Day 2 is social studies and geography. This class also has two teachers: a content area social stud-ies/geography teacher and a support teacher. Again, the two teachers have planned together for her. Assignments, textbooks, and assessments have been designed for her. After social studies she goes to health class and then to lunch. After lunch she has either art or a tech education class. Her last class of the day is a self-contained special education English class. Here she improves her read-ing, composing, and speaking skills. Again her goal is to be ready to enroll in an English class in 9th grade. Day 2 ends with homeroom and dismissal.

Support teacher #4 begins his day with students with whom he has made ap-pointments and students who seek him out for organization, clarification, or tu-torial (Figure 1.6). Some students come to complete tests they did not finish the previous day. Others want clarification on last night's homework. Still others have standing appointments, every Monday, for example, to confer with him on the progress the student has made on a long-term project or on a behavior modi-fication contract. On day 1, these morning appointments are followed by a series of meetings with 12 teachers. These teacher liaison meetings are possible be-cause 25% of the teaching staff is always free during one block. He uses these meetings to gather information about his students' current grades, the students' progress on long-term projects, and about upcoming assignments that might re-quire tutorial or adaptive education. He often has quick, miniplanning sessions with one or more of these teachers when a question about a student's behavior or the appropriateness of specific assignments and assessments is discussed. At 10:05 he has a preparation period. He may prepare liaison reports (compilation of the information from the teacher liaison sessions) to send to parents or to use at a conference with students on day 2. (See Appendix J for these report for-mats.) Lunch follows the preparation period. At 12:10 he sees students for whom individualized testing has been requested. He reads tests, scripts an-swers, cues memory strategies, serves as a listener, and paraphrases questions and directions. He also may teach students test-taking strategies such as elimi-nating options. (See Appendix L for test taking.) If he has no tests scheduled, he uses this time to observe students in the classroom. After the testing period he has a cooperative planning session with the social studies/geography teacher with whom he will teach on day 2. He ends his day with a few students who need behavior contracts signed or assignment notebooks checked.

On day 2 he again begins his day with students with whom he has made ap-pointments and students who seek him out for organization, clarification, or tu-torial. On day 2 his test administration period is at 8:35. After the test period, he cooperatively teaches a social studies/geography class with a 6th grade teacher. This is followed by lunch and a preparation period. His last block is spent meet-ing with teachers to gather information, plan lessons, and share ideas. He ends

FIGURE 1.6. MIDDLE SCHOOL SUPPORT TEACHERS ALTERNATE DAY BLOCK SCHEDULE USING A PARTIAL INCLUSION MODEL

Homeroom at the beginning and end of the day, 2 lunch/activity periods.

Times	Learning Support Teacher #1		Blocks
	Day 1	**Day 2**	
8:00–8:30	Student Appointments & Liaison		**Homeroom**
8:35–10:00	Preparation Period	CoTeach Soc. St. & Geo–8th	**1**
10:05–11:30	Special Ed. Math Instruction	Preparation Period	**2**
11:35–12:35	Co-plan for Soc. St. & Geo–8th	Teacher Liaison Meetings	**Lunch and Activities**
12:40–1:10	Lunch		
1:15–2:50	Learning to Learn	Special Education Math Instruction	**3**
2:55–3:00	Student Contact and Student Liaison		**Homeroom**

Times	Learning Support Teacher #2		Blocks
	Day 1	**Day 2**	
8:00–8:30	Student Appointments & Liaison		**Homeroom**
8:35–10:00	Co-teach 8th Science	Preparation Period	**1**
10:05–11:30	Sp. Ed. English & Reading–6th	Sp. Ed. English & Language–7th	**2**
11:35–12:35	Co-plan & Liaison 8th Science	Teacher Liaison Meetings	**Lunch and Activities**
12:40–1:10	Lunch		
1:15–2:50	Preparation Period	Special Ed. English & Language–8th	**3**
2:55–3:00	Student Contact and Student Liaison		**Homeroom**

Times	Learning Support Teacher #3		Blocks
	Day 1	**Day 2**	
8:00–8:30	Student Appointments & Liaison		**Homeroom**
8:35–10:00	Co-teach Soc. St. & Geo–7th	Co-plan Soc. St. & Geo–7th	**1**
10:05–11:30	Co-plan Soc. St. & Geo–8th	Co-teach Soc. St. & Geo–8th grade	**2**
11:35–12:05	Lunch		**Lunch and Actvities**
12:10–1:10	Teacher Liaison Meetings	Learning to Learn	
1:15–2:50	Preparation Period	Preparation Period	**3**
2:55–3:00	Student Contact and Student Liaison		**Homeroom**

Times	Learning Support Teacher #4		Blocks
	Day 1	**Day 2**	
8:00–8:30	Student Appointments & Liaison		**Homeroom**
8:35–10:00	Teacher Liaison Meetings	Individualized Test Administration	**1**
10:05–11:30	Preparation Period	Co-teach Soc. St. & Geo–6th	**2**
11:35–12:05	Lunch		**Lunch and Activities**
12:10–1:10	Individualized Test Administration	Preparation Period	
1:15–2:50	Co-plan Soc. St. & Geo–6th	Teacher Liaison Meetings	**3**
2:55–3:00	Student Contact and Liaison		**Homeroom**

his day with a few students who need behavior contracts signed or assignment notebooks checked.

At the high school level, the alternate-day schedule follows the same pattern as the middle school model. Students attend four 90-minute classes on the first day or week and four different classes on the second day or week. The models in Figures 1.7 and 1.8 have three lunch periods. A school that requires only two lunch periods could choose to have an extended homeroom period similar to those shown in the middle school models in Figures 1.5 (p. 12) and 1.6 or an activity period in the middle of the day.

The schedules shown in Figure 1.7 demonstrate the progression of a student through four years of high school as she moves from partial inclusion, with most of her classes in the shelter of the support classroom, to full inclusion. As she begins 9th grade, she is mainstreamed for half of her school day and is given support in the learning to learn block on day two for those courses in which she is mainstreamed. The focus of the special education classes and the learning to learn class is to teach her the skills she will need to be an independent learner. She is taught how to use her strengths and bypass her weaknesses, to advocate for her learning needs and accommodations, and to master the basic skills necessary for independence. Her ability to use technology such as computers and calculators is stressed.

As a 10th grader she increases the number of her mainstreamed courses by enrolling in a general math class that prepares students for algebra and stresses the use of technology as learning aides. A support teacher is in her general math classroom as a cooperating teacher every other day. In addition, she is still supported in her other mainstreamed courses through the learning to learn class that she attends every day.

When she enters 11th grade, she enrolls in one additional content course. She now attends special education classes only for English instruction. All of her other courses are with her peers. She continues to be supported in those classes through the learning to learn class, which meets every day. Her new mainstreamed course United States Cultures is cooperatively taught by a support teacher and a social studies teacher.

As she begins her senior year, she is fully included in the high school's courses. She attends a learning to learn class every day to receive the support services she needs to be successful and to prepare her senior portfolio project. She ends her day in a supervised work-study experience in a nearby daycare facility.

If the student is unable to be fully included, the schedule will most likely remain constant for four years. The time frame used for 9th grade can be used to schedule 10th, 11th, and 12th grade supplanted courses.

FIGURE 1.7. HIGH SCHOOL SPECIAL NEEDS STUDENTS ON AN ALTERNATE-DAY BLOCK SCHEDULE

Moving from Partial to Full Inclusion—3 Lunches

Times	9th Grader		Blocks
	Day 1	**Day 2**	
8:00–8:10	Homeroom		**Homeroom**
8:15–9:45	Special Education English	Special Education Social Studies	**Block 1**
9:50–11:20	Art	Special Education Math	**Block 2**
11:25–11:55	Lunch		**Lunch**
12:00–1:25	Physical Science	9th Health/PE	**Block 3**
1:30–3:00	Learning to Learn	Computer Processing	**Block 4**

Times	10th Grader		Blocks
	Day 1	**Day 2**	
8:00–8:10	Homeroom		**Homeroom**
8:15–9:45	Special Education Social Studies	General Math	**Block 1**
9:50–11:20	Basic Biology	Crafts	**Block 2**
11:25–12:50	Child Care	Special Education English	**Block 3**
12:55–1:25	Lunch		**Lunch**
1:30–3:00	Learning to Learn		**Block 4**

Times	11th Grader		Blocks
	Day 1	**Day 2**	
8:00–8:10	Homeroom		**Homeroom**
8:15–9:45	Learning To Learn		**Block 1**
9:50–10:20	Lunch		**Lunch**
10:25–11:55	Algebra I Fundamentals	Special Education English	**Block 2**
12:00–1:25	Environmental Education	U.S. Cultures	**Block 3**
1:30–3:00	Art II	Music	**Block 4**

Times	12th Grader		Blocks
	Day 1	**Day 2**	
8:00–8:10	Homeroom	Homeroom	**Homeroom**
8:15–9:45	Earth/Space	Consumer Math	**Block 1**
9:50–11:20	Learning to Learn & Senior Portfolio		**Block 2**
11:25–11:55	Lunch		**Lunch**
12:00–1:25	Citizenship and Responsibility		**Block 3**
1:30–3:00	Work-Study—Child Daycare		**Block 4**

Figure 1.8 shows the schedules of the teachers who support the student in her move from self-contained support classes to full inclusion. In this particular model, the support teachers have specialized in one grade level. If a school district has fewer than four support teachers, this model might not be possible.

Teacher #1 begins each day picking up the tests that need to be administered in an accommodated format. He, along with teachers #2 and #3, have divided the staff and each visits three to five teachers to pick up tests. These tests are stored in a locked file cabinet near the learning to learn classrooms where the teacher who will administer the tests will pick them up when the special needs student arrives to take the test.

FIGURE 1.8. HIGH SCHOOL SUPPORT TEACHERS' ALTERNATE-DAY BLOCK SCHEDULE

Moving from a Partial Inclusion to Full Inclusion Model—3 Lunches

Times	Learning Support Teacher #1—9th Grade Support				Blocks
	Day 1		Day 2		
8:00–8:10	Test Pickup				Homeroom
8:15–9:45	Special Education English		Special Education Social Studies		1
9:50–11:20	Preparation		Special Education Math		2
11:25–11:55	Lunch				Lunch
12:00–1:25	Co-teach Phy. Sci.	Co-plan & Liaison	Co-teach 9th Eng.	Co-plan & Liaison	3
1:30–3:00	Learning to Learn		Preparation		4

Times	Learning Support Teacher #2—10th Grade Support			Blocks
	Day 1		Day 2	
8:00–8:10	Test Pickup			Homeroom
8:15–9:45	Special Ed. Social Studies	Co-teach Gen. Math	Plan Math & Liaison	1
9:50–11:20	Teacher Liaison Meetings	Preparation Period		2
11:25–12:50	Preparation Period	Special Education English		3
12:55–1:25	Lunch			Lunch
1:30–3:00	Learning to Learn	Learning to Learn		4

(continued)

Times	Learning Support Teacher #3—11th Grade Support				Blocks
	Day 1		Day 2		
8:00–8:10	Test Pickup				Homeroom
8:15–9:45	Learning to Learn		Learning to Learn		1
9:50–10:20	Lunch				Lunch
10:25–11:55	Teacher Liaison	Preparation Period	Special Education English		2
12:00–1:25	Learning to Learn	Teacher Liaison	Co-teach US Cult.	Co-plan & Liaison	3
1:30–3:00	Preparation Period		Teacher Liaison	Preparation Period	4

Times	Learning Support Teacher #4—12th Grade Support				Blocks
	Day 1		Day 2		
9:50–11:15	Learning to Learn & Senior Portfolios		Learning to Learn & Senior Portfolios		2
11:20–12:50	Lunch				Lunch
12:55–1:25	Co-teach Citizenship & Responsibility (12th English & Govt.–Economics)				3
1:30–2:55	Co-planning	Prep. Period	Prep. Period	Teacher Liaison	4
3:00–4:15	Work-Study Supervision				Work-Study

On day one, teacher #1 teaches a self-contained, special education English class. The students are primarily 9th graders. Students are taught bypass strategies such as how to prepare referenced notes for use on tests, how to use graphic organizers as pre-writing or test-taking tools, or how to request help. The reading selections are from science and social studies texts as often as they are from works of literature. After English he has a preparation period and then lunch.

After lunch he teaches a physical science class with a content teacher every other time the physical science class meets. On the alternate days he cooperatively plans for the English class he teaches with a content teacher or has a liaison meeting with the content teachers who are at preparation or study hall periods. He ends his day with a class that is a mix of 9th and 10th graders. The students complete tests begun earlier in the day, use assignment notebooks to plan the evening's homework and begin that work, conference about the liaison information that was gathered from their content teachers, get behavior contracts completed, and receive tutorial support.

On day two he begins his day by picking up tests. He then teaches a special education social studies class followed by a special education math class. Once again the focus of both classes is on preparing students for inclusion. Bypass strategies are taught for those disabilities that are not remediable. The correct use of a hand-held calculator or the word processor might be stressed for those students who are unable to recall basic computation facts or spelling rules while problem solving or composing. While the text for social studies could be western civilization, the course content emphasizes how the strategies for conferencing, responding to feedback, and conflict resolution were used historically so that the students can practice those skills.

After his two special education courses, he goes to lunch and then cooperatively teaches a 9th grade English course on alternate days and cooperatively plans physical science or has liaison meetings. On day two he ends his day with a preparation period.

Support teachers #2 and #3 follow similar schedules of learning to learn and special education classes interspersed with cooperative teaching, cooperative planning, and teacher liaison meetings. Teacher #2 has mostly 10th grade students and teacher #3 has mostly 11th graders. As the students take more mainstreamed classes, the teachers spend less of their time in self-contained support classrooms and more time in liaison meetings or cooperative teaching and planning sessions.

Support teacher #4 works primarily with seniors. Her school day begins with block 2 because she has a work-study block that extends her school day. She has no support classes because all seniors are fully included in the school's courses of study. She begins with a learning to learn class that provides tutorial support, test accommodations, strategy instruction, and supervision of senior portfolios. Some of her students come to this class daily. Others only report to the learning to learn class on alternate days.

Following the learning to learn class, she has lunch and then cooperatively teaches an integrated English and social studies class called Citizenship and Responsibility. This class has three teachers—English, social studies, and support teacher #4. These same three teachers have a common planning period on day 1 during which they share liaison information and plan for the class. On day two, the support teacher meets with other content teachers to gather liaison information. At 3:00 she begins her extended day as a work-study supervisor. She meets with employees to review student progress and makes phone calls to arrange for employment opportunities in the community. She meets with students in the work-study program to develop résumés and practice job application and interview skills.

ALTERNATE-DAY BLOCK SCHEDULING FOR INCLUSION: CONCERNS

- ◆ Balancing student workload may require hand scheduling (not computer scheduling) for students who need support.

- ◆ Students are still required to pass six to eight courses in a year and to carry all courses for the full school year.

- ◆ Failed courses cannot be made up until summer or the following year.

- ◆ Balancing liaison meeting, cooperative teaching, and planning periods while providing supplanted and support instruction may require additional support teachers.

BENEFITS OF BLOCK SCHEDULING FOR SUPPORT TEACHERS AND STUDENTS

Moving from traditional schedules to block scheduling requires support teachers to reexamine their role in the education of their students. The traditional model of a support teacher with a small, intimate group of disabled and needy students or gifted students working together behind closed doors in a nurturing environment is possible only to a very limited degree. It becomes paramount for the support teacher to work cooperatively with the content teacher to plan, teach, assess, and monitor student progress. The support teacher must see his or her goal as preparing students for independence. Properly done, the benefits of inclusive education in a block scheduling format far outweigh the losses. Some benefits of block scheduling for support teachers and students needing supportive services are:

- ◆ Students have fewer classes to organize and prepare for daily;

- ◆ Students have extended time for processing and constructing for meaning;

- ◆ Students and teachers can confer during content classes;

- ◆ Students can receive rapid, direct feedback during content classes;

- ◆ Students with learning difficulties become part of, rather than separate from, the group;

- ♦ Students can be active participants in content classes and have appropriate support;

- ♦ Students can practice independence with feedback and a safety net in place;

- ♦ Students can retake failed courses in the same school year, if a 4/4 block schedule is used;

- ♦ Students have extended time for processing information for enrichment and in-depth learning;

- ♦ Support teachers can monitor and assess student progress during general education classes;

- ♦ Support teachers can observe students in authentic settings and accurately assess their need for specific strategy instruction;

- ♦ Teachers can plan together for extended periods, sharing the work and reducing teacher isolation.

The form that support takes varies. Instructional Support Teams (IST) or support teachers often cooperatively plan and cooperatively teach with content teachers. Reading teachers can collaborate with content teachers to plan for increased student comprehension of subject matter. Teacher aides and paraprofessionals can help do some more routine classroom practices under the direction of the content teacher. When two teachers consult with each other for the benefit of their students, both teachers share the responsibility for student achievement and success (Thomas & Grimes, 1985). In some cases, the support teacher and the content teacher share the power in the reciprocal interaction as opposed to the medical model where the consultant has the knowledge (Schon, 1987).

As student populations become more diverse, content teachers will find reliable, practical support from the support teachers in their buildings. As schedules are modified to accommodate teaching in the block, support teachers will program for consistent instruction for students in the content teacher's class. All students, including the nontraditional learner, will benefit from the extended learning time. Thus, the needs of all learners can be met and the school can provide challenging, authentic curricula.

2

TEACHING VERSUS COVERAGE

CONSTRUCTING MEANING

In many schools success is measured by how many students know the correct answer instead of how many students understand the concept. The curriculum is held to be absolute and content teachers are reluctant to revise it, even when students do not demonstrate understanding of the concepts being taught. The tests and activities are designed to measure the students' retention of facts rather than the students' understanding of the relationship between the ideas and concepts taught. Little attention is paid to application outside the classroom. It is assumed that the student will understand the fundamental principles of the course by memorizing the factual information. Under this traditional system of teaching and learning, students who do not memorize well, or who lack independent, analytical abilities, or who do not transfer skills from one course to another suffer.

How often do students say, "You didn't teach this," or "I don't remember doing this." Chemistry teachers can be heard wondering aloud why they have to reteach basic algebra when they know it was part of the math curriculum that preceded their course. Social studies teachers question why their students' written language mechanics are so poor only to hear the English teacher say, "I taught it. He got a B." These are common scenarios when teaching for transfer is ignored.

Teaching for near and far transfer is essential for training students to gradually acquire new skills and to apply those skills in new and unique settings. Near transfer requires the teaching of new skills and the guiding of students in the application of those skills in the same class setting, using content similar to that of the initial lesson. Far transfer occurs during the same class setting, or soon after, with content different from the initial skill session.

Learners who don't see relevancy in what they are asked to memorize or who do not see a practical application to what is being taught receive the low grades. The learner with needs is particularly vulnerable to this type of teaching and learning, as Robert Sternberg (1997) wrote:

> The consequences of this system are potentially devastating. Through grades and test scores, we may be rewarding only a fraction of the students who should be rewarded. Worse, we may be inadvertently disenfranchising multitudes of students from learning.

Many content teachers justify this teacher-dominated practice because of the pressure to "cover" the content in their respective curricula or by claiming that students need to know facts before they can understand concepts. As a result of this practice, students are not actively engaged in the learning process. Learning is passive and students soon become bored. This situation is exacerbated by block scheduling unless content teachers adopt more creative pedagogy (see Chapter 4) and jettison some less critical, low-level, recall information that their courses have traditionally emphasized.

To teach effectively in a block schedule, the content teachers, in cooperation with the support teachers, must first critically evaluate what they are teaching and how they will engage the learner in the construction of meaning. This task analysis should result in identifying those concepts that are critical to the understanding of their discipline and those intellectual strategies that must be taught to enable students to think productively about those concepts. In addition, by attending to the learning-to-learn schema, teachers can insure a higher engagement rate. Teachers familiar with the current research in language arts and constructing authentic meaning will be familiar with the concept of schema. The motivation to learn schema can be taught. Schema is a network of connected insights, skills, dispositions, and values. Schema enables students to engage in academic activities to accomplish their learning goals. They must use metacognitive awareness and think about the strategies they use in their attempt to learn schema. (See Appendix A for an example of a goal-setting schema).

CRITICAL, IMPORTANT, OR MERELY DESIRABLE

Task analysis, the process of breaking down assignments into components, allows teachers to identify the strategies and skills students will need to learn to meet successfully the demands of the curriculum. To aid in this task analysis the following format is helpful:

Clue Model

C = Critical (understanding big ideas)

L = Learnable (age/ability appropriate)

U = Usable (easily applied outside the classroom)

E = Expandable (does it evoke more questions and ideas)

Distancing Question: What do I want my students to know a year from now that is CLUE?

Concepts: What key words/concepts do I want my students to know a year from now and why?

Generalization: What big ideas that are CLUE do I want my students to know and why?

Skills: What skills that are CLUE do I want my students to know a year from now and why?

Big Questions: What questions that are CLUE do I want my students to know a year from now? What do I want my students to explain, analyze, interpret, evaluate, and in what role/context should they demonstrate this ability?

(Al Rowe, Iowa City, Iowa Schools, 1996)

Another way to analyze the curriculum is to use guiding questions:

♦ Is the topic sufficiently complex to elicit multiple problem-solving approaches? (Oversimplification can lead to boredom.)

♦ Is the topic relevant? (Lack of relevancy prevents engagement and impedes transfer.)

♦ Does the topic occupy a critical position in a hierarchy of content, so that the students must master it in order to understand important ideas that follow? (Inability to master this concept can result in failure.)

♦ Is this topic integrative? (The topic transfers easily to other topics or to the lives of the students.)

♦ Are national standards addressed by these topics? (Experts accept these topics as critical.)

Besides using structuring questions, content teachers should also consider what they can do to foster student movement toward the highest critical think-

ing skills. Working at the evaluative stage enables the students to process information at the highest stage of cognitive processing. It is also because of the sophisticated nature of the work that the students will most likely be engaged and
motivated. This brings the students far beyond memory of only minute,
course-specific facts. Curriculum and instruction that motivate must be rigorous and thought provoking. Skimming the surface of content is usually unambiguous and will not demand engagement. Cooking a Greek meal when studying ancient Greece will provide entertainment, but it does not engage students'
attention nor motivate students beyond the meal. It is necessary to provide
more than facts or entertainment to draw students to the work and away from
the distractions of adolescence and to sustain the momentum of study. Analysis, synthesis, and evaluation are necessary for students to maintain a high level
of joy for the work as they see their school task through to the end.

Once the critical components have been identified, the focus of the cooperative planning team must shift to activating students' prior knowledge. The cooperative team must have a vehicle to decide what students bring to the concepts and skills the team will teach. The teaching team must plan time to
identify students' misconceptions about the concept and skills that might inter-
fere with their ability to construct meaning about the new material. For example, students with intolerant attitudes toward some ethnic groups may have
great difficulty evaluating appropriate public policy on immigration. To identify these misconceptions, the cooperating teaching team must provide many
opportunities for students to express opinions and to elaborate on their views.
This process allows the teachers to assess student understanding and to structure their lessons accordingly. Block scheduling, with its expanded time frame,
greatly enhances this process.

CHOOSING THE MOST EFFECTIVE TEACHING METHODOLOGY

Having decided what to teach, what to jettison, and what the students already know, the cooperating team must now decide the most effective methods
with which to deliver instruction. Content that is challenging and provocative
is more stimulating to work with than material that merely covers simple and
unambiguous concepts or skills. Because block scheduling provides extended
teaching periods, students can be challenged to think, to ponder, to imagine, to
create, or to invent. Students can see relevancy in what they are studying. They
can make connections between what they are learning and their own world and
experiences. The classroom assignments must be at the proper level of difficulty, must be developmentally appropriate, and varied enough to sustain interest if students are to engage in the process. Whenever possible, the activities
designed by the content teachers and the supports teachers need to be authen-

tic, real-life tasks performed like those performed by scientists, historians, newspaper editors, and judges.

Reporting on his findings from the Teaching for Understanding Project, Vito Perrone (1994) summarized the factors that encouraged students to become intellectually engaged in an activity:

♦ Students helped define the content.

♦ Students had time to wonder and to find a particular direction that interested them.

♦ Topics had a "strange" quality—something common seen in a new way, evoking a "lingering question."

♦ Teachers permitted (even encouraged) different forms of expression and respected students' views.

♦ Teachers were passionate about their work. The richest activities were those "invented" by the teachers.

♦ Students created original and public products; they gained some form of "expertness."

♦ Students *did* something—participated in a political action, wrote a letter to the editor, worked with the homeless.

♦ Students sensed that the results of their work were not predetermined or fully predictable.

The process of constructing meaning takes time and repeated opportunities to think critically about the topic. The classroom activities, assignments, and assessments must call for thoughtful analysis and synthesis, not for the repetition of memorized bits of information. Block scheduling, with its longer time segments, is more conducive to teaching for meaning than the traditional schedule. The longer blocks of time allow for implementation of creative structures of teaching such as seminars, concept attainment/formation, small group instruction, reciprocal teaching, adaptive education, and tutorials. There is more information on these structures in Chapter 4, "Delivery of Instruction." The short time periods found in traditional schedules cannot make effective use of many teaching structures that allow for the teaching of understanding. These structures require time for reflection, discussion, and revision.

Many content teachers fail to appreciate how the extended time offered by block scheduling can increase student achievement. These teachers do not realize that the teaching practices used in a traditional schedule do not transfer easily into a block schedule. To teach effectively in the block schedule requires more than merely covering more material, or allowing students to begin their homework assignments before the class period ends, or showing the entire movie instead of only a portion of it. Only by developing a wide variety of educational methodologies can content teachers teach effectively in the block schedule. The cooperative planning process will help these teachers increase their instructional repertoire. Figure 2.1 illustrates how the block schedule with its longer segments of time permits more innovative practices

FIGURE 2.1. PRACTICES COMPARED

Traditional Schedule	Block Schedule
Forces a tightly structured, generally nonalterable script	Encourages and accepts student autonomy and initiative
Promotes reliance upon textbooks and workbooks	Encourages the use of raw data and primary sources along with manipulative, interactive, and physical materials
Promotes low level drill and practice	Allows students to analyze, interpret, predict, and create
Relies upon summative feedback	Promotes formative feedback with time for revision
Encourages lecture, whole group, teacher-dominated instruction	Promotes student-centered structures
Promotes the assumption that mastering content results in higher-level thinking	Allows for the teaching of metacognitive strategies

Teaching the diversified learner in the block schedule demands that the content teacher re-examine his or her teaching role. During this self-examination, the content teacher should consider the content of his or her course. (Does this content truly reflect that which is critical to understanding the fundamental principles of the course?) The content teacher must also consider the intellectual strategies he or she will employ. (Do these intellectual strategies engage the student and allow for the construction of meaning?) Finally, the content teacher must consider his or her new role as collaborator with the support teacher. (Am I willing to let go of those practices that impede diversified learners from succeeding in school?)

3

COOPERATIVE PLANNING BETWEEN SUPPORT TEACHERS AND CONTENT TEACHERS

Teachers should view cooperative planning as collegial problem solving. This type of problem solving may not be possible outside the block schedule. With the restructuring of blocks of time, colleagues can come together with a shared purpose—the success of their mutual students. Though professionals may have worked together for years, the responsibility of cooperative planning will cast the relationship in a new light. Regular discussions will keep the teachers focused on unit and lesson planning. This relationship, as with any new relationship, will suffer through growing pains while it stretches to become more than it had been. Each party needs to be aware of the willingness and readiness of the other to progress forward.

Cooperative planning between the support teacher and the content teacher increases student learning in the block schedule. With different purposes in mind, inclusion provides many opportunities for collaboration. Together teachers plan units. They decide what concepts, topics, and strategies to teach. They design and modify assignments to make them more appropriate for a broad range of abilities. Both teachers can be involved in monitoring for success. This valuable collaboration will pass by some teachers because they are not familiar with the various types of cooperative planning that can occur. Historically, secondary teachers have been autonomous, sometimes even isolated; they have experienced neither the benefits nor the challenges of collaboration. Cooperative planning is a tangible, positive experience that can end the isolation teachers often endure. A staff member, already busy in implementing the many adaptations necessary to convert to a block schedule, may not take the time to recognize the assistance that can come from collaboration with another teacher. In block scheduling, 25% of the staff is free during a block and available to meet with a support teacher. Given the daily duties the support teacher has, he would be available to meet on an average, every four to eight days. More details about scheduling to include teacher liaison and cooperative planning are found in Chapter 1.

A school district's philosophy for supporting students with learning needs must be considered when moving to block scheduling. If the philosophy regarding students with learning needs is that the students will gradually, but systematically, move toward independence, and if the philosophy regarding more capable students is to provide enrichment activities for acceleration, the district needs to use their support personnel within the content classroom.

District philosophy or limited funding can influence the kind of inclusion model a district embraces. Both of these factors can also affect the degree of involvement the support teacher can have with the content teacher for both planning and teaching. The support teacher may have to split his or her time between teaching in support and co-planning and co-teaching in content classrooms. Collaboration may take place every other week instead of every week. This changes the amount of involvement, but the involvement is still worthwhile and should take place.

Collaboration, within the construct of block scheduling, involves professional educators whose purpose is to solve problems and impact positively on student learning (Margolis, 1990). This equality underscores the competence of both professionals.

GUIDELINES FOR COOPERATIVE PLANNING

Some guidelines for cooperative planning should be established so that both the support teacher and the content teacher share the responsibilities of instruction and assessment. Both teachers monitor the success of the students. Thomas & Grimes (1985) suggest the following as necessary ingredients for effective cooperative planning:

- ◆ Each professional must nurture positive relationships.

- ◆ Each professional must use effective communication strategies.

- ◆ Each professional must use good listening skills.

- ◆ Each professional has equal status; no hierarchy exists.

- ◆ Each professional must be actively involved during consultation.

- ◆ Each professional has the right to accept or reject suggestions. The goal is to help the student, not to win.

◆ Cooperative planning is likely to be successful if teachers who want to plan and teach cooperatively volunteer for or request the experience.

A shared inquiry can help build a collaborative model between the support teacher and the content teacher. Good questions can initiate, extend, and conclude the most effective planning sessions. This type of dialogue can provide prompts to initiate discussion. The goal is to begin to talk about what each professional brings to the table in terms of expertise, comfort, and areas for potential growth. These are examples of questions that provide a springboard for discussion about what both teachers value:

◆ What do you want to see happening consistently in your classroom?

◆ What classroom activities do you try to avoid?

◆ How do you know if your lesson is effective?

◆ What skills do you bring to a collaborative team?

◆ How do you use assessment?

LEVELS OF READINESS IN THE PROCESS OF CHANGE

Each party brings certain expertise to the cooperative planning session and each will have specific expectations for the session. Hall and Loucks (1972) provide valuable information for the support teacher concerning the levels of readiness at which the content teacher is functioning in the hierarchy, as he or she approaches "maintaining change of practice." Becoming competent in teaching diverse learners within a block schedule is a process, not a single decision to change practice. Support teachers need to be aware of what kinds of support (Figure 3.1 on the next page) the content teachers require as they work through the process of change. At each stage, the support teacher and the content teacher must evaluate the effectiveness of their actions. Their cooperative planning sessions should promote both collaboration and student achievement. Reflection on practice and accepting feedback must become integral components of the cooperative planning process. Just as students are better able to receive instruction at developmentally appropriate levels, so too teachers adapt to change and adopt new methods at their individual stages of readiness.

At the nonuse level, a content teacher may show little concern about or involvement with the innovation of teaching a diverse learner in a block schedule. At this stage, teachers must hear the positive comments from the faculty members who are already actively engaged in the process. The content teacher may question others in the building about planning in collaboration with a support

FIGURE 3.1. SUPPORT FOR LEVELS OF READINESS TO ADOPT CHANGE

LEVEL	Content Teacher Behavior	Learning Support Specialist Response
Nonuse	Shows no involvement; passive or active resistance	Shares positive comments about the change
Orientation	Seeks answers to personal concerns	Provides direct, specific answers to inquiries
Preparation	Questions personal competence, contribution	Recognizes progress and contribution
Mechanical	Seeks ways to be efficient, productive	Shares what others are doing
Routine	Seeks out or is willing to use specialists	Provides task analysis and best practice information
Refinement	Focuses on student achievement	Shares expertise about planning, assessment, etc.
Maintenance	Recognizes personal success and achievements	Encourages sharing with others

teacher. The teacher may question how teaching diverse learners in a block schedule will affect them.

As teams of teachers become more comfortable with collaboration, the focus shifts from the collaboration process to student achievement. The planning teams will want clarification and redefinition of their roles. Their planning efforts will revolve around personal concerns.

As teachers begin formal collaboration, the following kinds of questions will be heard:

♦ What will cooperative planning and cooperative teaching be like?

♦ What can they expect?

Next, support teachers and content teachers will become uncertain about the demands of collaboration in the block schedule. Teachers often become unsure of their competence to meet the new demands. They question their roles, they perceive conflicts, and they wonder about their personal commitments. The support teacher must find opportunities to recognize the progress made, and to reassure the content teachers about their students' progress.

As the collaborators' practice becomes more routine, their needs will change again. Content teachers will consider the resources of the support teacher at this time. Together they will decide how best to use information and resources that are available to them. Collaborative support can address efficiency, organizing, managing, scheduling, and time demands. The collaborating teachers should focus on self-questioning as a guide for continuous movement forward. The questions the content teacher and support teacher now ask are:

- ◆ Are we using co-planning time in the most efficient way possible?

- ◆ Is there a better way to organize and analyze the data we are collecting about student growth?

- ◆ Is the management of resources, materials and information sufficient for maximum student achievement?

- ◆ Is there anything that can be done to insure the best use of the collaborators' time?

Finally, at the refinement stage, teachers are ready to look at the effects of collaboration in the block and examine the effects of this innovation on student performance.

- ◆ Are the students doing better?

- ◆ Are they becoming more competent?

The collaborators have a need now to monitor, collect data, and to examine student achievement. Discussions between the collaborators centers on reexamination of assessment procedures and of what they are teaching.

In the final phase, the expertise is now transferable from one content teacher to another. Teachers will recognize the successes in their own practice and in the practices of others. A real need for professional exchange occurs at this stage. Content teachers and support teachers demonstrate a willingness to mentor and to share their successes. Ultimately, content teachers will refocus the strategies for instruction, guided practice, and assessment shared through the collaborative planning experience and improve instruction for all students within the block schedule.

VARYING INSTRUCTIONAL METHODOLOGY

Increasing the variety of educational methodology is at the core of restructuring. Instructors must meet a variety of learner needs and styles while they find ways to increase student achievement. The students must learn to generalize and then transfer knowledge and processes to novel events within each discipline and beyond. A framework that provides the structure is shown in Figure 4.4, p. 70.

Knowledge of Bloom's (1976) taxonomy is very helpful if the teacher is to bring the instruction of "higher order thinking skills" to a conscious level. Co-planning teams must work actively to support analysis, synthesis, and evaluative levels of thinking rather than the coverage of material at a knowledge level alone. Academic content is what students think about—the who, what, when, and where are the facts of any course. The challenge is to go beyond the factual level by teaching and modeling so students analyze the critical attributes of the topics, generalize those attributes, and come to conclusions about how those patterns exist in similar situations.

TASK ANALYSIS

During the cooperative planning phase, the support teacher and the content teacher might use task analysis to break critical performances into discreet parts. The teachers examine the task requirements or the task demands that students must use to demonstrate understanding. The purpose of task analysis is to delineate the inherent steps involved in completing a cognitive task so the steps can be taught in a logical sequence. It also allows the teacher to identify at what point in the process learning breaks down for a particular student.

Initially, the steps involved in task analysis appeared in *Teaching Exceptional Children* (Frank, 1973). The process was used primarily in the instruction of special education students and in writing behavioral objectives.

- ◆ State a learning task.
- ◆ List steps, processes, or prerequisite skills needed to meet the task.
- ◆ Place steps in logical teaching sequence.
- ◆ Determine what steps a student can and cannot do.
- ◆ Teach the steps in sequence.

Since that time and in the newer context of thinking skills, task analysis was further operationalized (Beyer, 1991). "Reflective analysis" is accomplished by following these three major steps:

- ◆ Define the skill.
- ◆ Do it. Carry out all that is necessary to complete the task.
- ◆ Describe what was done mentally as the skill was carried out.

The following is an exchange between the content teacher and the support teacher as they discuss an English objective:

Content Teacher: I want students to detect bias in news stories.

Support Teacher: Let's discuss the skill and see if we can identify the most critical attributes in that skill.

Content Teacher: Well, they will first read the selection. As they read it, they must look for words that show bias.

Support Teacher: Let's make sure that the selection they are reading is at an appropriate level. We don't want the material to be so difficult to read that decoding takes all the students' efforts. We need material that will allow the students to move beyond simple decoding to comprehension.

Content Teacher: Yes, and they will also have to recognize the words that are emotionally charged enough to convey bias. It's the subtleties of language that will be difficult for John. He is a very concrete thinker.

Support Teacher: They should read and write the phrases that they think prove bias and check them against a rubric for bias. Maybe in the beginning I could provide a list of the more subtle words.

Content Teacher: Do you think I should create the rubric or should they?

Support Teacher: I think you can teach them how to create standards that constitute bias. Then the students will be working at the evaluative level of thinking. This will take a little more time and attention in the beginning but should pay off later.

Content Teacher: Yes, I think with instruction, most can do this step.

Support Teacher: Then for the last step, the students would compare the words they read against the standards for bias and decide what bias existed in the document.

A formal task analysis is also helpful when examining the assignments teachers are considering giving to students. Figure 3.2, developed by John Cradler (1986) as a way to judge computer software's thinking skill component, is a useful tool to have available during cooperative planning sessions. Its application extends beyond use with software alone.

Using any task analysis can focus the content teacher's attention on the discrete behaviors that an assignment might require, help content experts identify what specific skills may need to be taught directly, and distinguish the major emphasis or critical component of the unit or lesson from the incidental or merely desirable components. The list also can serve as a prior skill checklist. If a student is struggling with an assignment, a more basic skill may have to be retaught.

FIGURE 3.2. TASK ANALYSIS

What the unit (lesson) requires students to do:	Major	Minor	Incidental
Perceiving: 1. Observe carefully 2. Recognize things, ideas, events 3. Recall/remember things, ideas, events			
Conceiving: 1. Compare/contrast 2. Group/label (assign a descriptive label after grouping by attribute) 3. Categorize/classify (group according to label provided)			
Sequencing/seriating: 1. Motifs (recognize or identify the scheme or standard of arrangement) 2. Pattern (arrange things/ideas by an established, repeated scheme) 3. Order (arrange according to time, alphabetical order, size, etc.) 4. Priorities (arrange things/ideas by degree of importance)			
Analyzing: 1. Question (formulate relevant information) 2. Discriminate fact from opinion 3. Discriminate relevant from irrelevant information 4. Discriminate reliable from unreliable sources of information 5. Recognize part to whole relationships			
Inferring: 1. Understand the meaning of statements 2. Identify probable causes and effects 3. Use generalizations to solve problems or justify decisions 4. Make predictions 5. Identify one's own assumptions or those of others 6. Identify personal point of view or point of view of others			

What the unit (lesson) requires students to do:	Major	Minor	Incidental
Logical reasoning: 1. Use inductive reasoning (combine an assumption or a hypothesis with provided information to draw a tentative generalization) 2. Use deductive reasoning (draw a conclusion that can be proven by using only the information provided)			
Creative thinking: 1. Demonstrate fluency (produce a variety of responses) 2. Demonstrate flexibility (try several different approaches or apply a concept, idea, rule to a variety of situations) 3. Demonstrate originality (produce novel, unexpected, related responses) 4. Elaborate (extend or expand on a concept or idea) 5. Spontaneity (create new ideas/rules to fit available information—the "Aha!" experience)			
Problem solving: 1. Make decisions/judgments (draw conclusion to determine what to do after discerning and comparing relevant facts) 2. Define/describe the problem 3. Determine desired outcome 4. Search for possible solutions 5. Select and apply a trial solution 6. Evaluate outcome 7. Revise and repeat above steps (except #1) if desired outcome is not attained			

HIGHER-ORDER THINKING SKILLS

Far too many teachers teach thinking the way swimming was taught years ago. That is, they assign thinking tasks to students but give no direct instruction on how to do these assignments. That same technique was used to teach us to swim when we were tossed into a pond. Teachers have the obligation to deliver direct instruction to their students. This instruction should include how to think (Costa, 1991). Many teachers argue that students know how to think because they do it all the time, and they do. Nevertheless, requiring high-level thinking without providing instruction on the process or time for guided practice and reflection is, at best, shoddy.

In their race to cover material, content teachers leave little time for direct instruction on thinking skills and devote most of their efforts to covering content. Unfortunately, this practice is particularly prevalent among the student population that is the subject of this book. Content teachers sometimes presume that students who struggle in school can be successful only at a rote recall and recognition level of learning. Many teachers make assumptions about the cognitive abilities of the diverse learner that are not true. A balance needs to be made between the time spent on content and the time spent on how to process information at a high level. With direct instruction on how to process information at a high-thinking level, most students will be successful at the higher level. Traditional teaching will change only when teachers decide what is critical to teach and give themselves permission to jettison from their curricula the material that is not.

To teach the processes of high-level thinking, teachers must plan. This planning should include both the content teacher and the support teacher, and should involve answering these questions:

- In this unit, what essential questions, problems, themes, ideas, and generalizations will I have students develop?
- What questions or problems will I use as central starting points?
- How will the questions or problems be introduced?
- How will students collect, process, organize, and review data?
- What strategies for decision-making and problem solving will I model?
- How will students have an opportunity to answer questions and/or solve problems, draw conclusions, and evaluate results?
- What specific thinking skills will be explicitly taught?
- How will students process thinking used in this unit?
- What specific strategies will need to be taught?

It is also helpful to analyze what will be taught by asking what types of activities the students will be asked to do. Most classroom activities involve eleven basic categories. Lesson plans that include some of the following categories are found in Chapter 5 and in the Appendices:

- memorizing

- preparing for and taking objective tests

- organizing time and materials

- concentrating for a sustained period

- constructing for knowledge and understanding

- composing

- advocating for and taking responsibility for oneself

- solving computation and mathematical problems

- identifying key information

Many students who struggle with school need specific strategy instruction in one or more of these categories (Reid, 1993). All students benefit from having specific strategies for each area. Teachers must analyze existing curriculum to find what is worth having students spend time on and think about. That is, what in this course is worth remembering, understanding thoroughly, and transferring to other areas.

Block scheduling provides the opportunity for teachers to use their time to maximize student engagement in the processes of higher-level thinking. Because students are in classrooms for longer periods, the content teacher and the support teacher are better able to monitor the assignments, give additional instruction, and demand more sophisticated products. Teaching diverse learners does require planning specifically to support those students.

PYRAMID PLANNING

The Unit and Lesson Pyramid (Schumm, Vaughan, & Laval, 1995) can provide a framework to guide teachers in the often painful decision about what information, ideas, and concepts are critical to the course they are teaching and which are desirable and important, but not critical. This framework (Figure 3.3), developed by The University of Miami Project, asks teachers to look seriously at content units and daily plans and to decide what they will expect that all students learn. This basic information forms the largest section of the unit of instruction and contains the most important concepts and ideas. The information at the base level is more general than at succeeding levels. Once teachers determine critical information, the additional knowledge that most, but not all, students will master is identified. This is the desirable, but not critical, information of the course. This material includes extensions of the basic concepts, related ideas about the topic, and more complex concepts. Finally, the teacher decides what information, ideas or concepts are important to learn but will be mastered by only some of their students. This information is either more complex or more detailed and will be mastered by the smallest number of students. Using this format or framework allows the teacher to be very specific in planning for the success of a wide variety of students.

During co-planning, the content and support teacher can plan how to provide differentiated assignments. Inclusionary practices create classrooms where expectations for student achievement will vary from student to student. One student's best may be substantially different from another student's best. The acquisition of content skills and processes will differ for some students. The co-operating teachers may be able to vary the depth or the quantity of work for which a particular student is responsible. If fewer objectives, skills, and strategies are required, then assignments and guided practice activities also will be different for that student. The content and support teachers can decide together what are the most critical goals for which these students should be held accountable. The underlying philosophy behind differentiating instruction is that fairness does not mean that all students will be treated identically, but that all students are given what they need to be successful.

The authors of the unit planning pyramid suggest using a series of orienting questions to guide teachers through the planning and decision-making process. The lesson planning guides do not require extensive paperwork and are a routine that many teachers already use when planning. The first series of questions pertain to the topic:

Support Teacher: Is the material new or review?

Content Teacher: Some is review but most will be new. The students had some of the vocabulary in their course last year.

Support Teacher: What specific prior knowledge do you expect the students to have on this topic?

Content Teacher: Here are the material, concepts, vocabulary, and assignments they had last year. How complex and abstract are the new concepts going to be for the students with learning needs?

FIGURE 3.3. UNIT PYRAMID PLANNING

UNIT PLANNING FORM	Date _____ Class Period_____
What some will learn:	Unit Title: _____
What most students will learn:	Materials & Resources:_____
What all students will learn:	Instructional Strategies/Adaptations: ___
	Evaluation/Product: _____

Support Teacher: That isn't a simple question to answer. How clearly and at what reading level are the concepts presented in the textbook? And how can we relate this material to the previous instruction?

Content Teacher: I can offer the students at least two reading levels. We can pull some information off the Internet for the more advanced students. I'll make sure we have a reading level that is appropriate. I was thinking of tying the next unit to this one by....

Support Teacher: How important is this material to the overall curriculum?

Content Teacher: I think this section is critical. The students won't be successful next year if they don't learn....

The second set of guiding questions pertains to the teacher. If this teacher has students with learning needs, the answer to the final question in this series should include access to a support teacher as a cooperative planner and/or cooperative teacher.

- ◆ Have I taught this material before?

- ◆ How interesting is this topic to me?

- ◆ How much time do I have to develop this unit?

- ◆ What resources do I have available to me for this unit?

The final set of questions pertains to the students. This is the most critical set of information when teaching students with learning needs and should be the point in the planning process where a support teacher can offer the best planning information. A cooperative planning session might sound like this:

Support Teacher: Bill's learning needs make comprehension of the abstract idea of nationalism particularly difficult. Will his reading difficulties create a barrier to using the text independently?

Content Teacher: I'm confident that I can provide students with a variety of materials on several reading levels. I'm more concerned about maintaining the students' focus through these abstract ideas. Will students with attentional problems be able to concentrate on this material?

Support Teacher: We will need to provide a concrete structure to the unit. Perhaps guided notes or several types of graphic organizers (see Appendices C and D for examples of guided notes and graphic organizers) would make the material more understandable. The students with high interest in or prior knowledge of this concept should also be able to explore the topic in depth. We need to think of a way to have them share that knowledge with fellow classmates.

Content Teacher: The graphic organizers for cause and effect would work well. We can also set up a looseleaf model. Will the students have the vocabulary background they need for understanding?

Support Teacher: Not without some way to activate their prior knowledge. And don't forget, we have four students who are new to this school. They may not have had any of this vocabulary. I think we should preteach some of the critical vocabulary. Is there a way to relate this information to the backgrounds of the students?

Content Teacher: We could….

The authors of the planning pyramid stress two cautionary notes about using this planning routine. First, a student's learning needs do not automatically dictate his location on the pyramid. Because interests, prior knowledge and strategic skills will vary from topic to topic, they should not be locked into one level of the pyramid. All students should have access to all levels. Second, although a great deal of drill and practice may be necessary for some students to master the base level of a unit, this level should not be a long series of worksheets and drudgery. In the same spirit, the top level should not be associated exclusively with fun and exciting projects. When support teacher and content teachers plan cooperatively, appropriate and engaging activities, assignments, and assessments can be integrated into all levels.

LESSON PLANNING PYRAMID

The lesson planning pyramid also focuses on what content will be learned by all, most, and some students. This planning routine adds detail to what will be taught, how it will be taught, and identifies the processes the student will be asked to perform. The template provides a concrete tool for planning which promotes learning for all students (see Figure 3.4). As in the unit planning pyramid, the lesson planning pyramid begins with the identification of the critical, important, and desirable information of the lesson and is explicit about the content students will be asked to master. The content teacher and the support teacher then should consider the context of the instruction. The authors of the lesson planning pyramid suggest the following guiding questions:

- How will the school schedule, holidays, assemblies, and special events alter instructional time?
- How will the size and makeup of my class affect the teaching of the lesson?
- What grouping patterns are most appropriate?
- What role will the support teacher play in the lesson?
- What is the engaging nature of the material?
- What in-class and homework assignments are appropriate?
- How will the assignments be adapted for the students with learning needs?
- How will the students' learning be monitored at an informal level?
- How will the students' learning be assessed at the end of the lesson and unit?

FIGURE 3.4. PYRAMID LESSON PLANNING

Date: _____ Class Period: _____ Unit Period: _____

Lesson Objective(s): _____

Materials	Evaluation
In-class Assignments	**Homework Assignments**

LESSON PLANNING FORM

What some will learn:

What most students will learn:

What all students will learn:

Agenda

1._____

_____

2._____

_____

_____

3._____

_____

_____

4._____

_____

_____

5._____

_____

6._____

_____

7._____

_____

8._____

_____

FOCAL PLANNING

Focal planning is a second method of planning units of instruction that provides for the success of all students (Morocco, Riley, Gordon, and Howard 1995). This planning frame is more holistic than pyramid planning. When using this method of planning, teachers choose two students from the class, one student functioning at a high level of achievement and one functioning at a low level of achievement. Teachers plan units and lessons that allow for both students to be successful. This process, developed by the Education Development Center Project, provides a practical way to plan for the diversity of students in a class without having to plan for each individual. The content teacher and support teacher cooperate during the planning process to ensure the success of both a high-achieving and a low-achieving student at every stage in planning. This increased awareness leads to increased opportunities for all students. Content teachers and support teachers work together during the planning process to adapt the curriculum and instruction by integrating specific strategies and individual accommodations into the plan of instruction. The process of Focal Planning (Figure 3.5) uses this sequence:

♦ The content teacher brings the profile of a high-achieving student enrolled in the class to the cooperative planning session. The support teacher brings the profile of a low-achieving student to the planning session.

♦ Together the support teacher and the content teacher plan a theme unit that broadly appeals to the class, including the two focal students.

♦ Both teachers bear both students' needs and abilities in mind when selecting reading passages, and when developing assignments and specific writing activities.

♦ Both teachers plan to support the focal students so that both are fully engaged in the activities of the class. Some planning will be for the whole class. (All students will follow the events more accurately if we use a graphic organizer.) Other plans need to focus specifically on the focal students. (Dan will need to use an attention tape to stay focused during guided practice but John will be able to complete his practice quickly. John can extend his knowledge while others are completing the guided practice by completing....)

♦ Both the content teacher and the support teacher test and revise these plans as they observe the focal students during the lesson and as they assess the finished product. Both teachers can also assess whether the support and adaptations provided for the focal students were helpful for other students as well.

FIGURE 3.5. FOCAL PLANNING FORMAT

High	Low	Date_____ Class Period_____
Strengths	Strengths	Unit Theme_____ Materials and Resources_____ _____
Weaknesses	Weaknesses	Specially Designed Instruction/Accommodations: _____ _____ Extensions:_____ _____ Evaluation/Product:_____ _____

Observations:_____

_____

_____

DIRECT INSTRUCTIONAL MODELS

Block scheduling provides the opportunity for content teachers to shift their focus from covering material to teaching the process of learning. This can be done by introducing strategy instruction as part of their lessons using a direct instruction model. The strategies that allow all students to learn successfully can become a major emphasis of the teachers' lesson plan. The best learning strategies help all students learn how to learn and to become more independent. Strategy instruction has the additional benefit of allowing students with learning needs to bypass their weaknesses. For example, if a student has difficulty with his working memory and needs to empty his memory onto the margins of the test before attempting to answer the questions, a strategy for test taking called splashdown can be taught as part of objective test taking. (See Appendix L for the steps in the splashdown strategy.) Teaching this strategy directly to the class can allow the learning disabled student to bypass his learning disability and has the added benefit of teaching all the students an efficient test taking strategy. However, as every person who has learned touch-typing after using the hunt-and-peck method knows, adopting new ways of behaving requires repetition, intensity, commitment, and structure. Students who are accustomed to behaving in a passive manner may be resistant. Content teachers, who are highly knowledgeable in their subjects, may not have the same extensive knowledge about strategies. Support teachers may not be highly knowledgeable in a specific subject but have a wealth of knowledge about strategies for learning. Many of the tasks assigned at the middle and high school level combine several complex skills, all of which may need to be taught explicitly. During cooperative planning sessions, both areas of expertise can be tapped.

A major concern of content teachers is what to do with an extended block of time. During the cooperative planning sessions, the support teacher can play an important role in supporting the content teacher's shift of focus, from covering material and information to teaching the process of learning through the direct instruction of strategies, by identifying the specific strategies the students will need to use. The information in Figure 3.6 (p. 50) can aid in the identification of the type of strategies that would be supportive to the students.

This approach requires content teachers and support teachers to identify students' strengths and to do what Edwin S. Ellis (1995) calls "Watering Up" the curriculum. Expectations for all students must remain realistic but high. It is the work of the teachers, during cooperative planning sessions, to identify the frameworks, strategies, materials, and processes that will need to be directly taught to support all students in a challenging curriculum. An example of such a unit and a lesson using a pyramid planning framework is found in Figures 3.7, p. 55, and 3.8, p. 56.

The next example (Figure 3.9, p. 57) is a lesson planned using the focal planning framework. This is a two-day lesson used to introduce a science unit on evolution. The students are instructed in how to determine a scale and are assigned to groups. The groups research specific periods of time to discover what existed on earth during their assigned time. Each biologic, atmospheric, and geological event is written on a note card. The students then use the scale (1 foot = five million years) to place the cards in their relative places on the walls of the school's halls. Finally, the entire class travels the time scale to understand the concept of geologic time.

FIGURE 3.6. RECOGNIZING LEARNING NEEDS AND CHOOSING APPROPRIATE STRATEGIES

Problem Student Type	Indicators	Teacher Behavior	Student Strategies
Failure Syndrome: These children are convinced that they cannot do the work. They often avoid starting or give up easily. They expect to fail, even after succeeding.	1. Easily frustrated 2. Gives up easily 3. Says, "I can't do this."	1. Negotiated agreements 2. Specific proximal goals 3. Feedback stressing success 4. Efficacy training	1. Contracting 2. Goal setting with feedback 3. Coping strategies (time management, memorizing, test taking) 4. Self-determination strategies (I messages, positive self-talk)
Perfectionist: These children are unduly anxious about making mistakes. Their self-imposed standards are unrealistically high, so that they are never satisfied with their work even when they should be.	1. Work must be perfect 2. Fearful/frustrated with the quality of the work 3. Holds back from class participation	1. Understanding, approval, and empathy 2. Honor motivation 3. Offer support to maximize achievement	1. Goal setting 2. Self-assessment 3. Diagnostic thinking—rubric for success 4. Realistic feedback
Underachiever: These children do a minimum to just "get by." They do not value schoolwork.	1. Indifferent 2. Minimum work output 3. Not challenged by school work, poorly motivated	1. Realistic skill assessment 2. Value education and learning 3. Confront, persuade 4. Empowering and enthusiastic	1. Establish purpose 2. Goal achievement 3. Monitor comprehension (paraphrasing, predicting, etc.) 4. Strategies for all subjects and reflection on their use

Problem Student Type	Indicators	Teacher Behavior	Student Strategies
Low Achiever: These children have difficulty, even though they may be willing to work. Their problem is low potential or lack of readiness rather than poor motivation.	1. Difficulty following directions 2. Difficulty completing work 3. Poor retention 4. Progresses slowly 5. Poor abstract reasoning	1. Extra time, repetition 2. Value on working hard, not happiness 3. Effort and progress are required 4. Work is acceptable as long as the student applies him- or herself	1. Bypass strategies (cued notes, calculators, spell checkers, graphic organizers, guided notes, editing partners) 2. Strategy more important than content (reading, study, positive self-talk, requesting help) 3. Realistic self-assessment 4. Charting progress
Hostile-Aggressive: These children express hostility through direct, intense behaviors. They are not easily controlled.	1. Intimidates/ threatens 2. Hits, damages property 3. Antagonizes, hostile 4. Easily angered	1. Avoid engagement 2. Enforce limits and consequences 3. Positive relationships	1. Professional help 2. Behavior management 3. Socialization strategies (accepting feedback, conferencing) 4. Self-control strategies (dealing with frustration, managing anger)

(continued)

Problem Student Type	Indicators	Teacher Behavior	Student Strategies
Passive-Aggressive: These children express opposition and resistance but not directly. Difficult to tell if the resistance is deliberate. Often misdiagnosed as immature or attention seeking. Miscellaneous in form but exasperating in effect.	1. Subtly oppositional-stubborn 2. Controlling, borderline compliance with rules 3. Mars property 4. Disrupts surreptitiously 5. Drags feet	1. Recognize accurately, follow up with strategies 2. Offer support but refrain from doing for this student 3. Recognize anger but don't overreact to it	1. Problem solving and problem investigation strategies 2. Support strategies (requesting help, following directions) 3. Socialization strategies (accepting feedback, conferencing)
Defiant: These children resist authority and engage in power struggles with teacher. They want to have their way and not be told what to do.	1. Resists verbally—"You can't make me." 2. Derogatory statements about teacher to others 3. Resists nonverbally—frowns, mimics teacher, looks away, laughs at inappropriate times, deliberately does what the teacher says not to do	1. Ignore and avoid as much as possible 2. No powerful responses 3. Functional relationship 4. Environmental engineering	1. Professional counseling 2. Negotiated contracts 3. Strategies for responding to others
Peer Rejected: These children seek peer interaction and acceptance but are rejected, ignored, or excluded.	1. Forced to work, play alone 2. Lacks social skills 3. Picked on or teased	1. Positive group identity 2. Classroom as a learning community 3. "We..." statements	1. Socialization training 2. Strategies that target the undesirable trait

Problem Student Type	Indicators	Teacher Behavior	Student Strategies
Immature: These children have poorly developed emotional stability, self-control, self-care abilities, social skills and/or responsibility.	1. Exhibits behavior associated with much younger children 2. Cries easily 3. Loses belongings 4. Frequently helpless, incompetent, and/or dependent	1. Emotional support but not low expectations 2. Cueing 3. Value on behavior changes	1. Self-determination strategies 2. Self-reflection strategies 3. Problem solving strategies
Shy-withdrawn: These children avoid personal interaction, are quiet and unobtrusive, and do not respond well to others.	1. Quiet and sober 2. Does not initiate or volunteer 3. Does not call attention to self	1. Expect slow change 2. Comfortable, secure classroom 3. Indirect pressure to change—invitation and encouragement 4. Cueing and shaping behavior 5. Environmental engineering	1. Self-concept support—I messages, positive self-talk, eye contact 2. Group projects 3. Study partners—peer note takers, editing partners 4. Attention control strategies
Processing disabilities: These children process information slowly or in unique ways. They may be disorganized or use different processing routes to organize information. They show an extremely strong learning style preference for one modality.	1. Discrepancies between class and test performance 2. Difficulty with timed tasks 3. Doesn't follow directions 4. Writing, answers, bookbags are messy and disorganized 5. Often unprepared 6. Struggles to remember	1. Spiral or scaffolding teaching 2. Transfer cues 3. Require organization but not *one* method of organization 4. Allow for extended time	1. Semantic mapping, graphic organizers 2. Memorization strategies 3. Strategies that use strengths and bypass weaknesses (use of computers for essays) 4. Self-checking strategies

(continued)

Problem Student Type	Indicators	Teacher Behavior	Student Strategies
Efficiency disabilities: These children do not finish assigned work. They do not monitor their work habits. They have difficulty coordinating the tasks needed to learn. They do not plan or check and begin work impulsively.	1. Slow to master strategies 2. Strong conceptual/reasoning skills 3. Clings to old habits 4. Inconsistent 5. Careless errors, lost work	1. Coordinate multiple processes 2. Pace need to use strategies in close succession or simultaneously 3. Enforce consequences and reflect on causes	1. Organizational strategies 2. Planning and self-checking strategies 3. Goal setting and achievement 4. Strategies for directed attention (rubrics, checklists) 5. Bypass strategies (calculator, computer)
Flexibility disabilities: These children have difficulty shifting flexibly among different approaches. They may struggle to prioritize and to focus on salient details.	1. Difficulty adjusting to new teachers, situations 2. Talks around issues, cannot summarize 3. Poor study skills 4. Poor reading comprehension	1. Scaffolding techniques 2. Clearly identify salient attributes of assigned work 3. Sequenced, direct teaching of strategies 4. Environmental/physical cues	1. Strategies for rapid retrieval 2. Self-reflection strategies 3. Study routines (Math Assault, 5 day test prep, SQRRR) 4. Summarizing strategies
Distractible: These children have short attention spans. They are unable to sustain attention and concentration. They are easily distracted by sounds, sights, movement.	1. Difficulty adjusting to change 2. Rarely completes tasks 3. Easily pulled off task 4. Moves at inappropriate times	1. Environmental and instructional support 2. Reduce demands for sustained attention 3. Proximity and eye contact	1. Strategy to monitor/control attention (assignment and grade tracking, cross off as you go, attention tapes) 2. Material and time management strategies 3. Carrels, turtle, behavior checklists

Based on Brophy (1996) and Meltzer (1992).

FIGURE 3.7. DIRECTION INSTRUCTION MODEL USING PYRAMID PLANNING

UNIT PLANNING FORM

Date: 1/27 to 2/15
Class: Period Block 2
Unit Title: Fundamental Principles of U.S. Government

Materials & Resources: textbook, supplemental readings, editorial cartoons, video, data in charts and tables, posters on three principles

Instructional Strategies/Adaptations: lecture—historical background

Simulation of Supreme Court decision-making process

Paideia Seminars—preparation for writing essay on constitutionality of War Powers Act or Line Item Veto

Strategy to be taught—graphic organizer (debate), objective test-taking cycle

Evaluation/Product:

All students—objective test, graphic organizer, editorial or political cartoon

Many students—a constitutionality essay

Some students—friend of the court brief or render a court decision

---

What some will learn:
—*Apply criteria of checks and balances to the War Powers Act of 1973 or the Line Item Veto to decide the constitutionality of either*

What most students will learn:
—*Analyze significant historical controversies about Federalism, Separation of Powers, Checks and Balances*
—*Analyze Supreme Court decisions related to these principles*
—*Evaluate the decision of US vs. Nixon*

What all students should learn:
—*Define principles of Federalism, Separation of Powers, Checks and Balances*
—*Give examples from history and apply the knowledge to a present day issue*
—*Find and report on example of a principle through a current event*
—*Analyze a political cartoon on one of these issues*

(See Appendix D for a model of a debate graphic organizer and Appendix F for the objective test-taking cycle).

FIGURE 3.8. A COOPERATIVELY PLANNED AND TAUGHT LESSON

Date: 2/8 Class Period: Block 2   Unit Period: Fundamental Principles of U.S. Government

Lesson Objective(s): Create and use a rubric to decide if a parliamentary system or a presidential system best fits the U.S.

Materials

Text
Handout—Madison quotation
graphic organizer blanks

In-class Assignments

Discussion of Madison quotation
Steps 1 & 2 of objective test-taking cycle
Prewriting conference

LESSON PLANNING FORM

> What some students will learn:
> —*Evaluate proposals to model U.S. Govt. after European parliamentary system*

> What most students will learn:
> —*Analyze the major arguments advanced by the critics and defenders of our system and the parliamentary system*
> —*Use the rubric to justify a position on a parliamentary system in the U.S.*

> What all students should learn:
> —*List the benefits and costs of using parliamentary system*
> —*Create a rubric to use to justify changing U.S. system of Checks and Balances and Separation of Powers to a parliamentary system*

Evaluation

Traditional quiz
Graded graphic organizer
Speech or essay defending position

Homework Assignments

Gather key information from handouts, quotation and text

Agenda

1. —*Collect homework worksheet on Separation of Powers and Checks and Balances*
   —*Introduce and discuss Madison quotation*
2. *Whole class brainstorm possible solutions to the dilemma pointed out by Madison*
3. *Study groups—decide on the criteria that should be used when deciding to change the Checks and Balances and Separation of Powers in the U.S. Govt.*
4. *Groups present criteria to class—class chooses top 5*
5. *Introduce debate graphic organizer, review steps which will be followed in using and grading rubric*
6. *Rewriting and objective test-taking cycle conferences*
7. *Assignment—using the rubric developed by the class and the information gathered on the debate graphic organizer, express your viewpoint on the best possible solution to the dilemma expressed by Madison*

(See Appendix D for directions on using graphic organizers and Appendix F for instructions for the objective test-taking cycle.)

FIGURE 3.9. FOCAL PLANNING FORMAT

Unit: Evolution		
High — Paul	Low — John	*Date:* January 23–24 *Class Period:* 3rd *Unit Theme:* How Big Is Old— Geologic Time Scale *Materials and resources:* Meter sticks, marking pens, tape, 6x8 cards *Specially Designed Instruction and/or Accommodations:* Secret signal—"How are you doing?" to cue attention; Give John's group fewer cards and the shortest hall *Extensions:* Have Paul research the earliest period, make him responsible for checking others' measurements when he has finished his own *Evaluation/Product:* Completed note cards, contribution to time line

Strengths:
  Fluency
  Accuracy
  Persistence
  Uses Analogies
  Questions
	Strengths:
	  Reality based
	  Uses Prior Knowledge
	  Fact based
	  Kinesthetic
	  Develops Questions
	  Artistic	

Weaknesses:
  Intolerant
  Low Risk Taker
  Needs Correct Answer
  Conventional
	Weaknesses:
	  Processing Speed
	  Inattentive
	  Auditory retention
	  Impulsive	

Observations: All students were more attentive when we checked in with them regularly. John seemed fine with 5 cards but may have been able to do more. Next time let students choose number of cards they can do. We could have tapped into John's artistic talent by letting him illustrate the cards. Paul could have been more challenged. Maybe we could include a written assignment for some students.

4

DELIVERY OF INSTRUCTION

IMPROVING STUDENT ACHIEVEMENT

As the cooperating teachers continue to work together during instruction, the question now moves from, "What do you want all children to be able to do?" to "How is it possible for all the children to achieve in the classroom setting?" The support teacher provides some answers through explaining, modeling, and reinforcing specific teaching methodology. If inclusion in the block is to be successful and students with learning needs are to be supported, research about best practices must support the methodology used by the cooperating teachers. The content teacher must use his or her expertise about the content. The support teacher must use his or her expertise about learning.

Seven of the most highly effective, research-based, generic practices shown to improve student achievement can be incorporated into an extended period of instructional time. The practices are more effective than traditional ones, showing 0.5 standard deviations in growth when compared with student achievement in traditional settings. Students with or without learning needs will benefit from these practices. They are generic enough to extend across science, social studies, mathematics, English, technology, health, and foreign language. These best practices should occur regularly during extended blocks of time. Cawelti (1996) states that the most substantial results in raising student achievement come from a combination of the following practices, applied over two to three years:

- ◆ Students achieve more when they complete homework. The positive effects of homework on learning can triple when homework is graded and commented on by teachers.

- ◆ Direct teaching is most effective when teacher talk involves the rapid presentation of new skills in small, task-analyzed steps. To be most effective, direct teaching must be followed by guided practice, monitoring, and corrective feedback. Teachers should administer weekly and monthly exams.

♦ Students are more prepared to construct meaning when advance organizers are used. Advance organizers (Ausubel, 1968) show students the relationships between past learning and present learning. They give students a road map for thinking about the upcoming lesson. Goal setting and pretesting can provide the same continuity for learning. (See Appendix A for an example of a goal-setting schema.)

♦ Student achievement is enhanced when classrooms are student centered. Students must be taught how to monitor and manage their own learning. Metacognition, being aware of what goes on in one's mind as one learns, allows students to set goals and maintain control over their achievement of those goals. During guided practice teachers should provide models and exemplars and encourage students eventually to act independently from them.

♦ Interactions among students are increased when cooperative learning structures are used. Self-directed student groups support and increase other student's learning. When lecturing is reduced and students are placed in small groups, more students are actively involved and willing to contribute.

♦ Some students are more successful when they receive tutorial education or adaptive instruction. For all students to learn the skills, strategies, and content, learning problems need to be identified promptly and remediated quickly.

♦ All students can be successful if lessons and instructional methodology are adapted to meet the needs of the learners. Adaptive education is a diagnostic-prescriptive practice that directs all of the learning experiences a student has during the school day. After careful diagnostic testing, the adaptations required for a student to be successful are clearly outlined.

INCORPORATING THE MOST EFFECTIVE METHODOLOGY IN AN EXTENDED PERIOD

A workable framework for arranging the learning activities for extended periods can be developed by combining the suggestions of Canady and Rettig (1995) with seven of the achievement-oriented practices cited by Cawelti (1996). Canady and Rettig divide the extended period into three segments: explanation, application, and synthesis.

By incorporating graded homework, advance organizers, teaching of learning strategies, tutoring, cooperative learning seminars, and adaptive education, students with specific learning needs have an increased opportunity to be successful. Utilizing reciprocal teaching, seminar approaches, and concept attainment rounds out the most effective structures a teacher can use to support an increase in student achievement for all learners.

Advance organizers are the plans for the lesson given to the students. Through advance organizers, all students become aware of the class itinerary and what is expected of them.

Learning strategies are taught in conjunction with content. They provide the metacognitive base that allows process to become as important as content. All levels of students are taught how to think about their own thinking.

Tutoring is the one-on-one or small group instruction that is necessary when students need direct instruction to catch up or to accelerate.

Cooperative learning is a teaching structure that provides for students to work together to accomplish a goal. Students are given specific jobs to do and are evaluated as individuals and as contributing members of the group.

Adaptive education is a schoolwide support system. When students need significantly different instruction for either remediation or acceleration, a specially trained teacher provides the instruction. This instruction often happens through title one, special education, gifted education, or English as a second language (ESL) teachers, or through the reading specialist.

Concept attainment is a concept and vocabulary-learning structure based on the premise that concepts are labels associated with images, sensations, emotions, and linguistic information. Its benefits include allowing for the teaching of generalizations through the progression of sequential patterns from concrete to abstract.

Seminar is a teaching structure that increases student interactions and that focuses students' attention on issue-based problem solving. Throughout the cycle of teacher question, student response, and peer acceptance or refutation, students are able to construct meaning based on content specific terminology.

The extended teaching block can be divided into three distinct teaching segments: explanation, application, and synthesis. The role the content teacher and the support teacher play in each of the segments differs. The major distinguishing feature between the two professionals is their perspective. The content teacher tends to focus on the class as a whole. His or her primary focus is on *what* information needs to be acquired, rehearsed, and demonstrated. He or she is concerned with the specific skills, information, content, vocabulary, and ideas that need to be learned as defined by the curriculum. The support teacher's expertise tends to focus on differentiation. Therefore, the support teacher concentrates on *how* individual understanding is acquired, rehearsed and demonstrated. He or she is more concerned about how information can be applied by creating opportunities, time, materials, and activities that enhance or maximize the acquisition of information. This differentiation is accomplished through methodology that charts readiness, cues students to access knowledge, monitors performance, provides corrective feedback, and provides for ongoing behavior control.

ADVANTAGES OF COOPERATIVE TEACHING

There are clearly significant advantages to cooperative teaching. The content teacher can give up the individualistic perspective that can sometimes lead to subjective interpretations ("You need to work harder," following a poor test grade). The support teacher can give up the individualistic perspective that can be developed when working with students in small isolated groups ("You are very attentive and cooperative. The algebra teacher must not be giving clear instructions."). Cooperative interdependence between the content teacher and the support teacher allows for planning, designing, and evaluating curriculum together. When diverse learners are included in block scheduled classes, many challenges are presented to the teachers involved. There will be students who need to accelerate and students who need remediation. A support teacher in a block schedule class can provide one-to-one assistance during all the segments of instruction in the extended period. Students with shorter attention spans may occasionally need separate instruction or smaller groups in which to work. The support teacher provides the additional instruction that is necessary. In student centered classrooms, pupils are engaged at higher cognitive levels. They will talk more and work actively in small groups. Two people can monitor levels of questions, levels of responses, and student involvement in group process better and more quickly than one person.

Some educators may teach in a setting that only permits occasional co-teaching. The academic levels of some students may be significantly low. Therefore, the amount of time the support teacher can spend in content classes is limited because they are teaching the objectives of the individualized education plan in the special education classroom. Under these conditions the learning specialist and the content teacher should collaborate to determine the most effective use of the support teacher.

Also, the support teacher can make suggestions for teaching activities in her absence. Efforts should be made to establish a consistent schedule even if co-teaching and co-planning can't occur as frequently as both teachers would like.

EXPLANATION: THE FIRST OF THE THREE EXTENDED LESSON SEGMENTS

Explanation (see Figure 4.1) is the first of the three extended lesson segments—explanation, application, and synthesis. The first job of the cooperating teachers during explanation is to reinforce previously learned information and activate prior knowledge by correcting homework and giving corrective feedback. If the responsibilities for these activities are divided, both teachers can provide the students with the goals for the lesson and the itinerary for achieving those goals. Teachers can present the new information and give strategy instruction.

Although roles during reinforcement/feedback will vary between the cooperating teachers, in general, the content teacher will:

- ◆ circulate among the students to answer questions
- ◆ correct homework
- ◆ record homework grades
- ◆ note readiness to move on to the next concept or skill
- ◆ identify students who need small group instruction or enrichment

During reinforcement/feedback the support teacher will:

- ◆ conduct small group "check and correct" sessions
- ◆ indicate what the previous night's homework should look like through exemplars and expert models
- ◆ use graphics and visuals to activate prior knowledge

In general, if the support teacher is unable to co-teach this lesson, the small "check and correct" sessions might be done in cooperative group format where the content teacher gives the students correct answers or exemplars for the students to check and justify their work to each other. The students could be asked to generate graphics and visuals to demonstrate current knowledge.

During objectives/focus the content teacher will:

- ◆ share the content objectives of the lesson with the students
- ◆ explain what teaching structures will be used during the lesson

During objectives/focus the support teacher will:

- ◆ provide manipulatives and/or visuals for learners who need more specific information
- ◆ circulate and assist students in locating the materials they need for the class

FIGURE 4.1. THE EXPLANATION SEGMENT OF A BLOCK SCHEDULE

Stage	Time	Agenda	What the Content Teacher Does	What the Support Teacher Does
Explanation	15 min	Reinforcement/Feedback: —Homework —Questions	1. Circulate among students to answer questions from homework, grade homework 2. Record homework grades 3. Note the general readiness to move to next stage	1. Correct through examples and exemplars 2. Lead small group "check and correct" sessions 3. Identify need for small group instruction
	5 min	Objectives/focus: —Pretesting —Advanced Organizers —Goal Setting —Share Itinerary —Identify Structure To Be Used: Reciprocal Teaching Small Group Instruction Seminar Concept Attainment Tutorial Instruction Adaptive Education Lecture	1. Share the objective or focus for the lesson/unit 2. Identify and explain the structure to be used	1. Post the course of events 2. Circulate and assist students in locating materials needed 3. Post events of lesson 4. Provide manipulatives or visuals
	20 min	Explanation/Instruction: —Strategy Instruction —Factual Content	1. Direct skill instruction 2. Deliver factual content information 3. Explain structure to be used	1. Teach strategies 2. Write notes on board 3. Prepare a model 4. Focus attention 5. Correct misinformation

During the last part of explanation, new information should be given, strategy instruction should be provided, or content review should be conducted. The practices the teachers use for this instruction should be student centered and demand a high degree of student engagement.

During explanation/instruction the content teacher will:

♦ direct the strategy instruction

♦ provide the students with factual, content information

During explanation/instruction the support teacher will:

- teach strategies
- provide exemplars for the students
- write notes on the board
- prepare model notes
- complete a model graphic organizer
- focus attention and correct misconceptions

In general, if the support teacher is unable to co-teach this lesson, the content teacher should choose explanation activities that do not require strategy instruction, or choose strategies that are already a part of the students' repertoire. The content teacher could also provide the models necessary for complete explanation.

As the explanation segment continues, the itinerary for the lesson should be shared with the students. The cooperating teachers will continue to provide different but necessary instruction.

APPLICATION: THE SECOND OF THE THREE EXTENDED LESSON SEGMENTS

Canady and Rettig (1995) call the middle segment in the extended period "Application" (see Figure 4.2). This is the most demanding time for the cooperating teachers. During this segment the cooperating teachers engage primarily in diagnostic teaching or "kid-watching." Each teacher examines student performance; the content teacher focuses on the whole class and the support teacher on the individual. The cooperating teachers identify those students who need to be pulled out for tutorial education or adaptive instruction, two types of catch-up instruction. Both structures are addressed more completely in Chapter 6. The cooperating teachers identify those students who would benefit from extension and enrichment. Both teachers can seize the teachable moment to cue students for near and far transfer of skills, strategies, and content.

Gordon Cawelti's research on best practices shows that activities during instruction must provide for the maximum amount of student interaction if teachers are to maximize learning for all students. This is not the time for teacher talk, but, rather, the time for students to take control of their own learning using exemplars and experts against which to compare and to check their performance, understanding, and behaviors. It is time for students to be engaged in guided practice and small group instruction. Students use metacognitive strategies and talk aloud (oral rehearsal) as they process and apply new skills and new content. The diagnostic teaching activities during this segment of the block should provide the cooperating teachers a window into the thinking processes of their students.

FIGURE 4.2. THE APPLICATION SEGMENT OF THE BLOCK

Stage	Time	Agenda	What the Content Teacher Does	What the Support Teacher Does
Application	30 min	Kid-watching: —Guided Practice —Group Work —Corrective Feedback —Checking Against Expert or Exemplar —Evaluation for Pull-out —Monitoring for Mastery —Teaching for Transfer	1. Read summaries 2. Chart for mastery 3. Document levels of thinking 4. Teach for transfer 5. Identify which students need additional instruction 6. Direct the pace of the lesson	1. Listen to oral summaries 2. Provide corrective feedback 3. Direct use of exemplar and models 4. Provide pull-out for content or strategy instruction 5. Cue for near and far transfers

Monitoring for mastery can be the focus of instruction during this segment of the block. The cooperating teachers can instruct for both near and far transfer. The teachers must teach students to recognize when and in what new settings the content, skills, or strategies are useful. Both cooperating teachers must check for understanding and give corrective feedback to students.

Every extended period within a block schedule must include opportunities for the students to practice the skill involved in the lesson. During this time the teachers can observe students to see which concepts, content, and strategies still need to be practiced in the presence of the teachers and which can be done independently. During this time the teachers provide corrective feedback that allows the students to move closer to working the skills and using the concepts at an independent level.

Roles will vary between the content teacher and the support teacher when they are kid-watching. During kid-watching the cooperating teachers continue to provide different, but necessary, feedback to learners, and note those students who are succeeding and those who are not.

In general, during application, the content teacher will:

♦ read written summaries

♦ identify those students who require more than quick, simple feedback

♦ chart who is mastering the material and who needs additional instruction and practice

- document level of thinking

- teach for transfer

During application the support teacher will:

- provide specific instruction for remediation

- listen to oral/expressive students summarize

- provide corrective feedback to those students who need it

- cue for near and far transfer

If the support teacher is unable to co-teach during this lesson, the content teacher could:

- pair more capable students with those who need remediation

- allow students who complete their work before others to listen to the oral/expressive students summarize

SYNTHESIS: THE THIRD OF THE THREE EXTENDED LESSON SEGMENTS

Canady and Rettig (1995) call the final segment of the lesson "Synthesis" (Figure 4.3). This segment can be broken into two sections: closure and improving comprehension/memory. During closure, the room is cleaned and materials are returned to their proper location. Homework, which will be graded, is assigned and explained. The cooperating teachers continue to provide different, but necessary, closure for learners and to utilize instructional methods that support retention and understanding of information.

In general, during the closure stage, the content teacher will:

- present homework

- circulate to check for understanding

- identify which students require specific remedial strategies during the next block to enable them to complete their homework at an independent level

During the closure stage the support teacher will:

- script homework assignments for visual learners

- provide the adaptive instruction and tutorial education

- direct attention to models

FIGURE 4.3. SYNTHESIS SEGMENT OF THE BLOCK

Stage	Time	Agenda	What the Content Teacher Does	What the Support Teacher Does
Synthesis	5 min	Closure: —Clean up —Homework assigned and explained	1. Present homework 2. Explain steps 3. Check for understanding 4. Identify need for pull-out	1. Clarify misconceptions 2. Script steps 3. Provide tutorial or adaptive instructions
	15 min	Improving comprehension/memory: —Summarizations by students & teacher —Begin homework —Clarifying questions	1. Begin the summarization 2. Listen to generalizations 3. Correct for part to whole comprehension	1. Reinforce specific rehearsal, organizational, and memory strategies 2. Listen to student summaries to identify correct match to steps in process

If the support teacher is unable to co-teach during this lesson, the content teacher could ask a student to make an immediate copy of the homework, using carbon paper, for the students who need to see a model. She might also ask for volunteers to run short tutorials for the students who would benefit from hearing the information again.

The cooperating teachers should keep in mind that students remember best what happens first and last in a lesson. The improving comprehension/memory segment of the lesson allows teachers to capitalize on a student's last moments in an extended block lesson. Students begin the assigned homework at this time. So that misconceptions and confusions can be corrected before students leave the class, students are encouraged to ask clarifying questions, to begin the work to demonstrate that the processes that they were taught are understood, and to seek out a teacher if confusion occurs. It is an excellent time to have students summarize what they have just learned and practiced.

In general, during the stage for improving memory and comprehension, the content teacher will:

♦ identify and direct the use of summarizers for closing the lesson

♦ listen to students, make generalizations, bring parts back to the whole

During the stage for improving memory and comprehension the support teacher will:

- ◆ teach comprehension and memory strategies (chunking, color coding, splashdown)

- ◆ ask students with learning needs to orally rehearse the steps or to summarize the key processes for completing the homework

The planning for the role differentiation during each segment in the block (explanation, application, and synthesis) should result in well-organized and well-choreographed lessons. The cooperating teachers should complement each other in expertise, and they should be able to work effectively with all the students in the class. An entire block lesson (Figure 4.4, on the next page) should flow naturally, allowing all students equal access to the educational process while providing appropriate support for the unique learning needs of a diverse student population.

FIGURE 4.4. A THREE-SEGMENT BLOCK FOR COOPERATING TEACHERS

Stage	Time	Agenda	What the Content Teacher Does	What the Support Teacher Does
Explanation	15 min	Reinforcement/feedback: —Homework —Questions	1. Circulate among students to answer questions from homework, grade homework 2. Record homework grades 3. Note the general readiness for next stage	1. Correct through examples and exemplars 2. Lead small group "check and correct" sessions 3. Identify need for small group instruction
	5 min	Objectives/focus: —Pretesting —Advanced organizers —Goal setting —Share itinerary —Identify structure to be used: Reciprocal teaching Small group instruction Seminar Concept development Tutorial instruction Adaptive education Lecture	1. Share the objective or focus for the lesson/unit 2. Identify and explain the structure to be used	1. Post the course of events 2. Circulate and assist students in locating materials needed 3. Post events of lesson 4. Provide tangibles or visuals
	20 min	Explanation/instruction: —Strategy instruction —Factual content	1. Direct skill instruction 2. Deliver factual content information 3. Explain structure to be used	1. Prepare a looseleaf model 2. Model graphic organizer 3. Focus attention 4. Correct misinformation

Stage	Time	Agenda	What the Content Teacher Does	What the Support Teacher Does
Application	30 min	Kid-watching: —Guided practice —Group work —Corrective feedback —Checking against expert or exemplar —Evaluation for pull-out —Monitoring for mastery —Teaching for transfer	1. Read summaries 2. Chart for mastery 3. Document levels of thinking 4. Teach for transfer 5. Identify which students need additional instruction 6. Direct the pace of the lesson	1. Listen to oral summaries 2. Provide corrective feedback 3. Direct use of exemplar and models 4. Provide pull-out for content or strategy instruction 5. Cue for near and far transfer
Synthesis	5 min	Closure: —Clean-up —Homework assigned and explained	1. Present homework 2. Explain steps 3. Check for understanding 4. Identify need for pull-out	1. Clarify misconceptions 2. Script steps 3. Provide tutorial or adaptive instructions
	15 min	Improving comprehension/memory: —Summarizing by students & teacher —Begin homework —Clarifying questions	1. Begin the summarization 2. Listen to generalizations 3. Correct for part to whole comprehension	1. Reinforce specific memory, organizational, and rehearsal strategies 2. Listen to student summaries for correct steps in process

5

TEACHING STRUCTURES

Certain teaching/learning structures open the curriculum for students with remedial, as well as enrichment/acceleration, needs. Several attributes mark these structures. First, they maintain high but appropriate expectations for performance. The emphasis is on enhancing students' strengths and the focus is on thinking-skill instruction. Second, they provide a variety of ways for students to gain and demonstrate knowledge. Participation, elaboration, and reflection through projects and activities are used. Finally, these structures provide integrated content and strategy instruction. This combination of content and strategy encourages active learning. When using these structures in a cooperatively planned and taught unit of study, the content teacher can provide the content knowledge and the content strategy instruction. The support teacher can provide the repetition, intensity, structure, and extensions that diverse learners require.

Previously, during the cooperative planning stage, the collaborating teachers would have chosen from among a variety of teaching structures such as reciprocal teaching, small group instruction, seminars, concept development/attainment, tutorial instruction, adaptive education, and lecture. Each structure is discussed in depth later in the chapter. All the structures are worthwhile, but some may be better than others depending on the learning goals . What the content teacher and the support teacher each does specifically during these teaching/learning structures must be agreed upon during co-planning.

During co-planning, the collaborating teachers must determine what teaching methodology will best carry out their instructional goals. During co-teaching the teachers work together to ensure that all students achieve those goals. Both teachers monitor achievement as the students analyze, synthesize, evaluate, and apply new content information. The students are taught strategies to check their own understanding of content and process. Teachers and students cooperate by creating rubrics, models, and exemplars to distinguish quality. The structures that follow allow for a high level of student engagement and have the potential to increase student achievement (Cawelti, 1996). Each of these structures is demonstrated in the agenda section of the pyramid planner (Figure 5.1, on the next page).

FIGURE 5.1. USING THE AGENDA PORTION OF A PYRAMID PLANNER

Date:_____   Class Period:_____   Unit: _____
Lesson Objective(s): _____

Materials	Evaluation
In-class Assignments	Homework Assignments

LESSON PLANNING FORM

What some will learn:

What most students will learn:

What all students will learn:

Agenda

Explanation (40 min.)

Reinforcement_____
Objective_____
Explanation_____

_____

_____

Application/Kid Watching (30 min.)

_____

_____

_____

Synthesis (20 min.)
Closure_____

_____

Improving Comprehension/Memory

_____

_____

RECIPROCAL TEACHING

Reciprocal teaching (Palincsar & Brown, 1984; Palincsar et al., 1993) is a method of delivering instruction that places less emphasis on teacher talk and more emphasis on interactive dialogue between students and between the students and the teacher. The emphasis is on teaching students a system of monitoring and regulating their comprehension of content material. Reciprocal teaching has the added benefit of being as useful in science and math as it is in

English and social studies. This method of delivering instruction in the block is relatively easy to learn and can be used successfully by students with a variety of learning styles.

During reciprocal teaching, students and teachers take turns leading discussions about the meaning of the content they are learning or the text they are reading. This interactive dialogue is structured around four basic strategies: summarizing, questioning, clarifying, and predicting. The four strategies, essential for comprehension, are taught directly to the students during the explanation/instruction stage, before the students are asked to use the process of reciprocal teaching independently. During the direct instruction of the four primary strategies, the content teacher and the support teacher serve as the expert models and the content is used as a vehicle for the strategy instruction. The initial content, therefore, must be chosen with extreme care and occupy a secondary role during the instruction of the four basic strategies. Once the students have mastered the strategies, the difficulty of the content material can be raised and students can use the strategies independently to comprehend the curricular information.

One benefit of reciprocal teaching is its flexibility of use in a variety of settings. This method of instruction can be used during one-on-one or small group sessions by the content or support teacher. It can be used for whole group instruction or during small group instruction. The techniques are easily understood and, when taught directly, easily mastered. The research done by Palincsar indicates that reciprocal teaching rapidly increased comprehension and that the comprehension was maintained over time and generalized to other situations.

A second benefit of reciprocal teaching is that it frees both the support teacher and the content teacher to engage in extended periods of kid-watching. By observing small groups of students or whole class discussions when the class is using reciprocal teaching, the teachers can detect how well students are comprehending. This method provides the opportunities for immediate and meaningful feedback in the subject the students are learning. Students who are struggling with one of the four strategies can be identified. If necessary, a single student or small groups of students with learning needs can be pulled out of the content classroom for more individualized remediation or subskill instruction. For more information on kid-watching, see Chapter 6.

Summarizing is the first strategy taught. During the explanation/instruction segment of the block, students are taught how to identify key information in the content being studied and to restate that key information in their own words. The content teacher should provide instructions in how to summarize. The support teacher may not be needed during this segment of the block.

During the kid-watching segment of the lesson, students practice summarizing key information. The students can summarize sentences, short paragraphs, or simple science and math procedures or concepts. The summarized mation is then checked for accuracy against the text or the expert model. (See Appendix G for a mnemonic device used to check for accuracy.) As the students gain proficiency, the difficulty of the content material is increased. During this phase, both the content and support teacher should be engaged in intense kid-watching. A cooperatively taught block period using the summarizing strategy during reciprocal teaching might look like the lesson shown in Figure 5.2.

FIGURE 5.2. SUMMARIZING STRATEGY DURING RECIPROCAL TEACHING

Structure: Reciprocal Teaching   Subject: Algebra I
Strategy: Summarizing   Content: Factoring

Stage	Time	Agenda	What the Content Teacher Does	What the Support Teacher Does
Explanation	15 min	Reinforcement/feedback: —Homework correction —Questions answered	1. Circulates, answers questions about homework on difference of two squares 2. Records the homework grades 3. Notes the general readiness to move to next stage	Leads small group "check and correct" sessions for finding greatest common factors and difference of two squares
	5 min	Objectives/focus: —Share itinerary —Identify reciprocal teaching as structure	1. Defines reciprocal teaching 2. Identifies comprehension as goal 3. Identifies text to be used and materials needed	1. Posts the course of events 2. Circulates and assist students in finding materials needed

	20 min	Explanation/instruction:
		—Content skill: factoring
		—Strategy: summarizing
		—Study aides
		    visual cues
		    mnemonics
			1. Instructs (factoring)
			—Details steps
			—Provides sample problems
			2. Assigns summary
				Provides strategy instruction
				—Details steps used in summarizing
				—Offers optional visual cue/mnemonic (foil or face)
				—Reviews oral expressive/visual expressive differences

Stage	Time	Agenda	What the Content Teacher Does	What the Support Teacher Does
Application	30 min	Kid watching: —Guided practice —Corrective feedback —Expert model —Evaluation for pull-out —Monitoring for mastery	1. Reads written summaries and makes suggestions for corrections 2. Charts students who have reached mastery—expert models 3. Identifies students who may need additional practice.	1. Listens to oral expressive students summarize 2. Provides corrective feedback to these students
Synthesis	5 min	Closure: —Homework explanation	Presents homework	Circulates to answer questions, clarify directions
Synthesis	15 min	Improving comprehension/memory: —Summaries by students —Begin homework	1. Begins homework as a check for understanding 2. Assigns students identified as expert models to be peer teachers	Writes on overhead as students retell steps and process of summarizing

Questioning, the second strategy to be taught directly after the class has mastered summarizing, reinforces the summarizing strategy. During the explanation/instruction segment of the block, students are taught how to generate questions by separating key information from the content and then posing that key information as a question. Students can then read to answer the question.

During the application segment of the block, the questioning can take place at many levels of thinking. Students can use questioning to find supporting details and simple factual information or to infer, apply, and extend information from the content being studied.

Clarifying, the third strategy in reciprocal teaching, is important for students who concentrate more on the process of decoding than on understanding as they read. During instruction in clarifying, students are taught how to recognize and respond to particular portions of the content that can cause poor understanding. During the application of this skill, a series of substrategies may need to be taught for those who stumble when faced with new vocabulary, unfamiliar wording, or difficult concepts. These substrategies include such processes as rereading, using context clues, judging the speed at which to read, and requesting help. The content teacher and the support teacher may need to group some students for specific instruction in these substrategies during the next explanation segment of the block. It is also possible that students with serious learning needs may need to be identified and pulled out of the content classroom for tutorial/remedial instruction in very specific substrategies. More information on the substrategies can be found in the adaptive education section of this chapter.

The final strategy is predicting. Students are taught to make judgements about what will happen next. Students are shown how to activate prior knowledge about the content being studied, to recognize and use the clues provided by headings and subheadings, and to structure questions around embedded information. The students then read to discover whether their predictions were well founded.

Content and support teachers who use reciprocal teaching may find it beneficial to learn more about:

- how heterogeneous groups function

- how to identify and use content vocabulary at high levels for discussion, but at simple levels for reading so students with reading disabilities are not at a disadvantage

- how to differentiate instruction to increase the difficulty of the course content

- how comprehension strategies can be varied to address many learning styles

SMALL GROUP INSTRUCTION

Peer grouping is another highly effective structure (Slavin, 1986) for classrooms of heterogeneously grouped students. Student learning groups place less burden on teacher-directed instruction. These group processes transfer the responsibility for learning (acquiring information, applying study skills, sharing ideas, listening to feedback, monitoring behavior) to the student. The use of small group instruction promotes the idea of the classroom as a community of learners. It gives the student the chance to view the whole as more than the sum of it parts and provides unique opportunities for the cooperating teachers to instruct and assess.

Peer-oriented learning groups can be created for a variety of purposes. These groups can be either teacher directed or student directed. Teacher-directed groups are structured to teach specific skills, to practice previously taught skills, or to teach specific subject matter. Student-directed groups are structured to complete an assigned project, respond to a challenging stimulation, or to prepare solutions to open-ended problems. Both of these groups are designed to promote responsibility for learning and individual accountability.

Small group instruction has many benefits for students. One benefit is an increase in the students' use of elaborative thought. A second benefit is that student talking and interaction is increased. A third benefit is that the students are exposed to a wider perspective when discussing material. Placing a concrete, practice student with an abstract, theoretical student requires both to learn and practice the art of compromise after some instruction on give and take. A fourth benefit is that students develop their interpersonal skills. Placing a nontask-oriented student with a task-oriented student, for example, provides an opportunity for the students to experience a real-life situation that requires them to learn and use appropriate interpersonal skills.

From the teacher's point of view, one benefit of small group instruction is the opportunity for teaching the strategies and skills necessary for students to function as successful members of a community. These opportunities occur in a natural, authentic way as an extension of the structure. Teachers can give instruction in strategies such as making a complaint, responding to anger, or accepting feedback during the best possible teachable moments. A second benefit of small group instruction is the opportunity for the content teacher and the support teacher to engage in kid-watching. Both teachers will have many opportunities to evaluate a student's growth in two areas: the use of group process, skills, and strategies and the mastery of the content. David Johnson (1996) suggests a "five-minute walk" through the class after the teachers select the particular skills to evaluate. The cooperating teachers can take varying routes through the room, gathering information as they stroll. Teachers can ask recall and comprehension-level questions as they walk through the classroom. If answers come from *many* or *all* students, the cooperating teachers know the information and strategies have been learned. If answers come from *some* or a *few* students, the cooperating teachers can decide if additional instruction is necessary. Rubrics, observations, checklists, and questioning can help the teachers determine a student's or a group's readiness to move on.

How to group students is the first critical decision teachers must make when using a small group structure. There is wide agreement among researchers that cooperative methods can have a positive effect on student achievement if the tasks feature both group goals (working together to earn recognition, grades, rewards, or other indicators of group success) and individual accountability (Kagan, 1992). When students work together to prepare a single worksheet or project without differentiated tasks, very little benefit in achievement is gained. Teachers working with heterogeneously grouped students in a block schedule need to design the groups to promote positive interdependence. One method of designing student groups is to make sure that each student brings a unique and important skill to the task and that each student has a way to be evaluated independently of the group's product. Thus, not only must the heterogeneous group be classified according to high, medium, and low abilities, but also the particular skills necessary for the successful completion of the academic and collaborative objectives need to be considered. Because the support teachers have diagnostic training and are familiar with formal and informal diagnostic tools, their expertise can be helpful in making decisions about the membership of the student learning groups. These teacher-made groups often have the best mix because teachers can put together optimal combinations of students. Members of the student groups have the best opportunity to foster positive interdependence based on each other's strengths and to offer help to the group's efforts.

At the beginning of the explanation segment of the block, students can be surveyed or pretested. Information pertinent to the student group task can be collected from each student. The results can be tabulated and used to assign students to heterogenous groups with as equal a distribution of skills as possible. Information such as learning style, technological expertise, and personal interests can be gathered and considered. Teams should be formed so that each student can assume some primary responsibility for the group's progress. Team members should be able to tap into an individual's strengths.

The objective/focus segment of the block can be extended to allow the groups to develop job descriptions with individual responsibilities clearly defined. A five-minute walk can be used to decide the readiness of the groups to function. If *all* students have clearly defined jobs and responsibilities, the cooperating teachers know the groups are ready to function. If only *a few* of the students have clearly defined jobs and responsibilities, additional time or instruction may be needed. The cooperating teachers may need to teach strategies (conferencing, accepting feedback, handling a complaint) directly to a group. Students who analyze quickly or who jump to conclusions may be intolerant of other's points of view. Students with learning needs may require explicit directions on how to respond to anger or criticism.

The explanation/instruction segment of the block can be used to teach the skills and strategies necessary for successful small group instruction. Assigning students to sit next to each other does not mean that they automatically become good communicators or group members. During this segment of the block, instruction on how to successfully conference needs to occur. Students need to know about types of conferences (discussion, problem solving, training, information gathering) and the steps and skills necessary to be successful when using conferencing as a strategy. (See Appendix H for steps to teaching for conferencing and the related strategy of accepting feedback and requesting help.) Conferencing provides the opportunity and format for teachers and students to interact on a one-to-one basis. Conferencing breaks the pattern of teacher as leader and presenter of information and student as follower and receiver of information. Using conferencing, teachers and students become co-investigators, co-learners of the content. Conferencing, as a strategy, can be used for a variety of purposes:

- to reinforce the skills used for critical and creative thought

- to provide guidance for students in their projects

- to keep students appraised of their progress

- to assess the students' knowledge of content

Asking students to express their thoughts aloud can externalize the thinking process and give both the speaker and the listener feedback on what has been understood and what is still only vaguely processed. Further, expressing ideas can serve as a catalyst for the creation of new ideas, and can force the speaker and listener to take in information in a way that cannot occur when working in isolation.

The application segment of the block is the most demanding and active time for both the content teacher and the support teacher when a small group structure is used. All conferencing groups will need practice and the freedom to make mistakes. The teachers need to monitor the progress of the conferring groups without interrupting the natural ebb and flow of group processes. During their five-minute walks, the cooperating teachers must offer advice when the groups are confused or stuck, and suggest alternatives to individuals or groups who have gone awry. It is essential, during this guided practice time, that the teachers serve as expert models on how to behave as a collaborator and have strategies available for dealing with the wide variety of interpersonal problems and skills deficits that will arise. At any time during this segment of the block there may be a need for pulling a few students aside and providing specialized, focused intervention and remediation. It is common to observe some students who tend to dominate conferences and others who are passive participants. The content teacher or support teacher can offer tutorial education through one-on-one direct instruction, through a software program, or through small group-teacher directed sessions. There may be a need for a pull-out time for students whose learning disabilities require intensive instruction. The support teacher can provide the necessary strategy instruction for the specific skill or process deficits that the student demonstrates. For example, the teacher might instruct the students in a peer-partner proofreading strategy so that students could improve the quality of their composition. This allows students to utilize each other's expertise instead of waiting for the teacher to act. (See Appendix I for editing partner process.) Thus remediation can occur with the groups or individuals who need it and the other students can benefit from continued coaching from the other cooperating teacher who can function as a traveling expert, offering instruction as the remaining students request it or need it. A cooperatively taught lesson on conferencing might look like Figure 5.3.

FIGURE 5.3. COOPERATIVELY TAUGHT LESSON ON CONFERENCING

Structure: Small Group Instruction   Subject: Health
Strategy: Conferencing (accepting feedback)   Content: Nutrition

Stage	Time	Agenda	What the Content Teacher Does	What the Support Teacher Does
Explanation	20 min	Objectives/focus: —Share itinerary —Structure: small group instruction —Pretesting	1. Identifies requirements of nutritious party planning group project 2. Distributes questionnaire	Circulates to answer questions about the questionnaire
	20 min	Explanation/instruction: —Strategy: conferencing Accepting feedback I messages —Content: five basic food groups recommended daily allowances	1. Reviews purpose, use of I messages during conferencing 2. Instructs in conferencing steps & job description requirements 3. Distributes conferencing and assignment rubric bookmark	Using questionnaire answers and previous knowledge of students—sets up student groups for nutritious party project
Application	30 min	Kid-watching: —Guided practice —Group work —Corrective feedback —Evaluation for pull-out instruction —Monitoring for mastery	1. Assign students to groups 2. Develop job description 3. Use a five-minute walk as diagnostic tool 4. Offer advice to groups or individual who are stuck 5. Instruct students who need individual remediation in group processes	

Stage	Time	Agenda	What the Content Teacher Does	What the Support Teacher Does
Synthesis	5 min	Closure: —Clean-up —Homework explanation	Assigns nutritious party project due dates and summarizes requirements	Circulates to collect job descriptions and answers individual or group questions
	15 min	Improving comprehension/memory: —Summarizers students teacher —Begin homework	1. Circulate among groups to assist in distribution of work to individual group members as requested or needed 2. Offer advice to groups on procedures as needed	

Content and support teachers who use small group instruction may find it beneficial to learn more about:

♦ how differences in learning styles can affect group progress

♦ how to use diagnostic teaching to identify weaknesses in students who are required to work collaboratively

♦ how to structure groups to insure individual accountability

♦ how to vary small student group formations

♦ how to use strategy instruction

SEMINARS

Seminars are student-centered teaching structures. They are beneficial for increasing student interactions during issue-based problem solving. The seminar format requires that teacher be both leader and facilitator. This presents a perfect opportunity for cooperative teaching between the content teacher and the support teacher. A second benefit of these seminars is that students are required to use high level questions and answers. The teachers should recognize this as a great opportunity to begin to collect data and measure the growth students will experience in their ability to use higher level thinking and to become increasingly self-regulated and self-disciplined.

The steps to using the seminar method are:

♦ The teacher asks an open-ended question or states a problem for examination.

♦ The students respond.

- The teacher raises additional core questions.

- This cycle of teacher questions/student responses and peer acceptance or refutation continues until the students arrive at a more general, more broadly encompassing understanding.

- The students are asked to write/prepare an essay on the seminar topic, compose a letter to the editor, or complete a lab report.

During a typical explanation segment of a block in a science lesson on photosynthesis using a seminar with a graphic organizer as a scaffolding device, the students listen to the itinerary of the class and learn how the seminar works. One graphic organizer that can be used is Gowin's Vee. (See Appendix D for examples of the Gowin Vee graphic organizer.) The content teacher provides this instruction on the use of the graphic organizer while the support teacher provides the visual model for the students.

During the application segment of the lesson the students comment and ask clarifying questions about the topic. They complete the information side of the graphic organizer. The content teacher provides the interactive dialogue using his or her knowledge base to guide the students while the support teacher completes the model graphic organizer as a visual record of the seminar. Students are assigned to work groups and use the knowledge activated by the seminar to design an experiment, solve a problem, or respond to a point of view. The teachers share responsibilities for the assessment of the students. The kid-watching might be divided. The content area teacher monitors the groups' progress, providing feedback as they establish their responses, ideas, and designs. Both teachers can identify students who may need tutorial education. The support teacher might chart individual student achievements, direct students' attentions to the models, and provide the tutorial education or adaptive education needed.

During the synthesis segment of the block, homework is assigned by the content area teacher. (Students summarize using the doing side of the graphic organizer to make predictions about the results of a science lab.) The support teacher checks each student's graphic organizer to insure the most critical information needed to complete the assigned homework is recorded. Both teachers provide the additional guided practice or clarification needed by some students.

The plan for this type of seminar using a pyramid planner, might look like Figure 5.4. The responsibilities of the teachers would have been discussed and agreed upon during cooperative planning sessions.

FIGURE 5.4. PLAN FOR A SEMINAR

Structure: Seminar Subject: Biology I
Strategy: Graphic Organizer (Gowin's Vee) Content: Photosynthesis

Date: 2/22/98   Class Block: 2   Unit: Photosynthesis
Lesson Objective(s): Students design lab to test effects of carbon dioxide and light on photosynthesis. Students will respond to the question: How will humans solve the problems of overpopulation through photosynthesis?

Materials	Evaluation
Gowin's Vee (handout and large model), *BioScience*, July-August 1992, pp. 490–93, Gowin's Vee rubric, test tubes, bromothymol blue, droppers, light source, straws	Score graphic organizer according to the rubric (see Gowin's Vee scoring rubric in Appendix D)

In-class Assignments	Homework Assignments
Participate in seminar, complete the knowing side of Gowin's Vee, plan a lab (focus questions, materials, procedure portion of Gowin's Vee)	Predict the results of the lab experiment designed during class

LESSON PLANNING FORM

What some will learn:
—Use one variable to design extended lab
—Explain the process of photosynthesis
—Evaluate lab accurately using rubric

What most students will learn:
—Complete the Gowin's Vee
—Develop a lab with controls and variables
—Recognize the components of photosynthesis
—Use a rubric for scoring

Agenda

Explanation (40 min.)

Reinforcement none **Objective** *Mr. Clark*: Check understanding of article—*Mrs. Lewis*: Visual

Explanation *Mr. Clark*: Explain seminar & Gowin's Vee, present the focus question: How will humans solve the problem of overpopulation?, conduct the seminar posing refuting comments and asking clarifying questions, assign student lab groups

Mrs. Lewis: Fill in knowing side of the model Gowin's Vee as seminar proceeds

(continued)

What all students will learn:
—Locate key information
—Activate prior knowledge
—Use a graphic organizer to gather information
—Sequence steps in photosynthesis

Application/Kid-Watching (30 min.)

Mr. Clark: Monitor lab groups' progress, provide feedback on lab designs, identify students who need tutorial or adaptive education, cue for on task behavior

Mrs. Lewis: Chart progress, provide exemplars, conduct CD-ROM tutorial, monitor bromothymol station

Synthesis (20 min.)

Closure *Mr. Clark:* Assign and explain the homework (predict the results of the lab you will do during tomorrow's block and complete the focus questions on the Gowin's Vee), *Mrs. Lewis:* Check that all students have recorded the most critical information on the Gowin's Vee

Improving Comprehension/Memory *Mr. Clark:* Answer content questions and monitor progress *Mrs. Lewis:* Provide additional guided practice

(See Appendix D for an example of the Gowin's Vee graphic organizer)

Content teachers and support teachers who use a seminar and scaffolding devices like the Gowin Vee may find it beneficial to learn more about:

♦ recognizing and using higher level questions

♦ using wait time

♦ designing lessons using scaffolding techniques

♦ constructing lessons using issue-based problem solving

♦ using small group instruction

♦ designing authentic instruction

♦ developing scoring rubrics

♦ learning and teaching through graphic organizers

Before this actual lesson begins, the students would have been given a reading, usually as homework. For example, they might have read an article on biotechnology and agriculture and have been assigned to highlight, or tag with a

Post-It, the portions of the reading they believed illustrated strong points. (See Appendix C for steps in teaching this strategy.) If any student had problems comprehending the text, the student would have been expected to have asked the support teacher for reading assistance before the seminar was held.

During the explanation segment of the block, the students could anticipate time for a quick review of the reading and their highlighted pieces. The students would be expected to use the text during the seminar to cite specific proof to support their points. During the application segment, the students would participate in the seminar. They would pose questions and make comments about the assigned reading. During closure, the students would synthesize what was learned during the seminar, summarize and write a paragraph.

A cooperatively taught social studies block using a Socratic seminar might look like the lesson shown in Figure 5.5.

FIGURE 5.5. A COOPERATIVELY TAUGHT SOCIAL STUDIES BLOCK USING THE SOCRATIC METHOD

Structure: Socratic Seminar
Strategy: Discussion

Subject: Social Studies
Content: Civil Liberties (4th Amendment)

Stage	Time	Agenda	What the Content Teacher Does	What the Support Teacher Does
Explanation	15 min	Reinforcement/ Feedback: —homework —questions	Circulates to respond to clarifying questions from students as homework is checked	
	5 min	Objectives/focus: —Share Itinerary —Structure: *Socratic Seminar*	Models levels of questions from knowledge to evaluation (see Appendix B for levels of questions)	
	20 min	Explanation/Instruction: —Rules for Socratic Seminar —Content instruction		

(continued)

Stage	Time	Agenda	What the Content Teacher Does	What the Support Teacher Does
Application	20 min	Kid-watching: —Guided Practice —Corrective Feed-back —Group work —Checking against model (teacher) —Monitoring for mastery	1. Records level of student engagement 2. Participates as needed to keep seminar moving, clarifies	Makes decisions about concepts and understanding
Synthesis	5 min	Closure: —Homework Explanation	1. Provides model of highlighted points from the seminar 2. Assists as needed with synthesizing ideas and writing summarizing paragraphs	Provides students with structures or oral rehearsal as aides for paragraphing
Synthesis	25 min	Improving Comprehension/Memory: —Summarizer: student —Begin homework		

Content teachers and support teachers who use a Socratic seminar may find it beneficial to learn more about:

- recognizing and using levels of questioning
- teaching for inductive/deductive reasoning
- responding to denotative/connotative meaning
- using wait time
- teaching through analogies
- using concept mapping
- facilitating versus teaching
- creating and using performance rubrics

CONCEPT ATTAINMENT

Concept attainment (Marzano, 1986) is a structure for learning concepts and vocabulary. It is based on the premise that concepts are labels associated with images, sensations, emotions, and linguistic information. To truly understand a concept, students must experience the concept's images, sensations, and emotions. Students move through a progression of sequential patterns from concrete to abstract to arrive at a generalization. Because it takes time to develop concepts, ample practice must be provided with each subsequent skill or concept. Teachers should be aware of students' current development and performance so that learning materials can match appropriate levels of thinking. Pretesting, goal setting, and activating prior knowledge can help with this.

The steps to learning this structure are:

♦ Step 1: Concrete

Students express what comes to mind when they think about a concept. This is a free exploration stage, a stage of discovery. During this stage, the teacher teaches the skill or concept to be learned. Graphic organizers, charts, manipulations, or other visual aids help make the lesson more effective. (See Appendix D for sample graphic organizers.) At the end of this step verbal explanation takes place. The students' prior knowledge is activated:

- What does the equation make you think of?

- How is this term like that term?

- How is this term different from that term?

- Do you recognize any familiar processes, skills, or terms?

- Where have you seen parts of this before?

♦ Step 2: Representation

At this stage the students use visual representations to supplement the verbal explanation. They identify critical concepts or steps and represent them in a summarized format. Oral rehearsal is one such format in that it allows the student to move back and forth from visual representation to symbolic representation with both models available. Students engage in active questioning and answering during this step.

- Step 3: Abstract

    At this stage, the students rely on visual imagery to recall both concrete and representational material. Through this imagery, the students begin to internalize thoughts and strategies.

- Step 4: Maintenance

    At this stage the students continue with guided practice and move toward the ability to transfer the skills in the same class session, as well as to a new setting, with greater independence.

The extended period of a block schedule can take full advantage of this teaching structure. During the explanation segment of the block, students can be exposed to the denotation of the vocabulary. They would also respond to questions that activate prior knowledge. They could use the oral rehearsal strategy by describing and correctly using the words for the process in which they are engaged. (Teachers of mathematics may recognize this strategy as math assault, which was introduced by Miles and Fozcht (1995). See Appendix D for the math assault strategy.)

During application, the students follow a model and practice. They seek out or accept feedback. They continue to write the steps in which they are engaged. By doing so, they they overlearn the language required to carry them through any process. By writing these steps, they can create a cue card that stays with them and is used for reference until memory takes over. During the application segment of the lesson, the students can be placed in small peer-study groups where they support each other in completing cue cards or using the cue cards in guided practice.

Some mathematics teachers may find that they have a more heterogeneously grouped class than they initially suspected. This can be dealt with very effectively if two teachers are working cooperatively. After the explanation segment of the lesson some students may naturally break out into smaller groups. It is possible that other students will need to hear the same instruction again. Others will be ready to do guided practice immediately. A third group can work at a higher level and do some enrichment activities after they complete a short guided practice. Both the content teacher and the support teacher might discuss how best they could address each of these small groups' needs, effectively dividing the work.

It is possible for the support teacher to continue making a valuable contribution during synthesis, the third phase of the lesson. During this phase, while the teacher is providing the structure for reflection, review, or reteaching, the second teacher begins to assess the work produced during the application phase. This assessment will enable the teacher to quickly note whose work is satisfactory and whose work requires additional attention later. This step is an important one because it can provide the preplanning for determination of the amount or type of additional direct instruction that may be necessary.

A lesson using concept attainment with two cooperating teachers might look like the lesson shown in Figure 5.6. Content teachers and support teachers who use the concept development/attainment structure may find it beneficial to learn more about:

- oral rehearsal (or other talk-aloud strategies)

- bridging teaching techniques

- using visuals in math instruction (see Appendix G for visual mnemonics for factoring)

- using manipulatives in math instruction

- task analysis

TUTORIAL

Tutoring (Cawelti, 1994) is a teaching structure that is highly effective in raising student achievement. It involves teaching one student or a small group of students who have specific instructional needs. Both peer tutoring (a proficient student works with a slower student) and teacher tutoring have yielded great benefits for students because this structure focuses instruction on very specific student need. Tutoring benefits students who are not able to keep pace with the rest of the class or who need short-term, repeat instruction in content or specific strategies. During all three segments of the block—explanation, application, and synthesis—the cooperating teachers can determine which students would benefit from individual or small group tutoring. The students themselves may even realize that they need remedial instruction.

- Step 1. The teacher identifies who needs tutoring (or the student requests tutoring).

- Step 2. The teacher provides instruction based on what the student needs to know using modeling and reinforcement.

- Step 3. The student practices the content and strategy in a controlled setting of tutoring.

- Step 4. The student returns to the whole group setting.

- Step 5. The teacher cues the student, when necessary, to bridge the tutorial to the whole group.

- Step 6. The teacher positively reinforces the application of the new content and strategy within the whole group setting.

FIGURE 5.6. A CONCEPT ATTAINMENT LESSON

Structure: Concept Attainment   Subject: Algebra I
Strategy: Oral Rehearsal   Content: Factoring

Date: 12/15/97   Class Block: 3   Unit: Factoring Trinomials
Lesson Objective(s): Students will factor trinomials moving from concrete to abstract reasoning

Materials	Evaluation
Blank 6x8 cards—one for each student Chart of concept attainment—stage 2	Match student generated cue card against model. Use cue card to factor trinomial completely.
In-class Assignments	**Homework Assignments**
Problem solving—10 factoring problems (page 123)	Use cue cards to factor trinomials on page 125.

LESSON PLANNING FORM	Agenda
 What some will learn: 1. how to teach others factoring without using cue card 2. how to explain process of factoring **What most students will learn:** 1. how to factor trinomials 2. how to construct a cue card without prompting	*Explanation* (40 min.) Reinforcement *Mrs. Bell:* Answer questions re homework, collect homework *Mrs. Combs:* Check & correct sessions, provides visuals and models objective *Mrs. Bell:* Factor trinomials using specific vocabulary of math assault *Mrs. Combs:* Circulate to direct attention, provide visuals Instruction *Mrs. Bell:* Verbalize steps for factoring-specific vocabulary, demonstrate steps while doing a sample problem *Mrs. Combs:* Record steps on board (paraphrasing Mrs. Bell) *Application/Kid-Watching* (30 min.) *Mrs. Bell:* Observe students paraphrasing steps for factoring as the students create 6x8 cue card, identify students who need tutorial, make suggestions to improve cue cards *Mrs. Combs:* Listen to oral paraphrasing and record students words on 6x8 cue cards, cues for near transfers, make suggestions for improvements to cue cards

| What all students will learn:
1. how to use oral rehearsal strategy
2. how to use math assault strategy
3. how to factor trinomials using a cue card
4. how to construct a cue card | **Synthesis** (20 min.)
Closure *Mrs. Bell:* Assign homework practice problems—restate steps *Mrs. Combs:* Circulate to check for accuracy in recording homework in assignment notebooks Improving Comprehension/Memory *Mrs. Bell:* Circulate as each student uses cue card to solve problems *Mrs. Combs:* Conduct tutorial |

(See Appendix D, math assault, for cue card used when factoring trinomials.)

ADAPTIVE EDUCATION

Adaptive Education (Cawelti, 1994) is a highly effective teaching practice that has its base in diagnostic-prescriptive instruction. Adaptive education uses a variety of instruction strategies. This practice, in reality, can be a complete school program. It can be the continuum of legally mandated special education placements that range from self-contained, full-time programs to part-time support programs. It can be individual tutorial or small group instruction that occurs in the content class when teachers co-teach. Some school districts make the commitment to provide adaptive education for non-special education students as well.

In this book, the curriculum for adaptive education is learning to learn. During the learning to learn block, the individualized education plan's goals and objectives are implemented. Delivery of the learning to learn curriculum requires a highly skilled teacher who is completely familiar with both formal and informal diagnostic procedures, planning, and task analysis. She needs an in-depth knowledge of and commitment to instruction and skill development through the teaching of strategies.

Ideally, instruction in each strategy should occur around academic content information and in context. The strategies for oral rehearsal, conferencing, summarizing, clarifying, accepting feedback, and scaffolding have been used throughout the sample block lessons in Chapter 5. It is also possible for teachers to teach what Meltzer (1992) calls "bypass strategies." If a student has a specific disability in memory and that disability is not correctable, then strategies are taught to the student that allow for compensation or bypass. Figure 5.7 shows one strategy, math assault, in the context of algebra.

The following steps should help guide strategy instruction. The steps are a task analysis of the principles of cognitive behavior modification used by Dreschler and Schumaker (1986) when working with low-achieving adolescents:

FIGURE 5.7. PLANS FOR ADAPTIVE EDUCATION IN A BLOCK SCHEDULE

Student: George Blunt		Date: Oct. 13, 1997 Class Period: 2
Expected	**Current**	*Strategy:* Math Assault *Materials and resources:* Blank 6x8 cards

Student will sequence steps to factoring trinomials on a 6x8 card.
 	
Student will use the Math Assault cue card to factor trinomials.
	Strengths:
	  Student can recognize the initial 2 steps to factoring trinomials.
	  Student is a strong auditory learner.
	
	Weaknesses:
	  Student has sequential memory deficits.
		Specially Designed Instructions:
		  Student will use cued note card during guided practice and assessment
		Evaluation/Product:
		  Student will match the cue card with 100% accuracy to model
		  Student will factor trinomials with 70–100% accuracy

Observations: George was able to follow the script when I prepared the card. He had considerable difficulty when he had to prepare the card without my auditory cues. Next time try preparing a tape and have George prepare the card from the taped directions. Once the steps were written, George had to be reminded several times to check his work against the card. He tended to dash ahead until he was confused before resorting to the reference card.

Step 1. The teacher pretests the student on the use of the strategy and has the student commit to learning it and using it.

Step 2. The teacher describes the strategy and how the strategy can be used to match the student's learning strengths and the academic content.

Step 3. The teacher verbally and behaviorally models the strategy.

Step 4. The student verbally rehearses the components of the strategy.

Step 5. The student practices the strategy in a controlled setting with positive feedback.

Step 6. The student practices the strategy in a specific academic content area with positive feedback

Step 7. The teacher demonstrates how the strategy will generalize to other settings.

The learning to learn curriculum in adaptive education tends to focus on strategic instruction in these areas:

- attention and concentration (attention tape, turtle, chairs in place, relax with black)

- comprehension: constructing for understanding (RAP, graphic organizers, muscle reading, SQRRR, stop and think, skimming)

- composition (graphic organizers, editor partner process, steal it, semantic mapping, revision strategy)

- math problem solving (math assault, three-column note-taking process)

- identification of key information (Post-It process, Cornell notes, note-taking partner, predicting test question process)

- memorization (key word pictures, peg words, mnemonics)

- organization of time and materials (assignment notebook process, materials checklist, ABC prioritizing)

- self-advocation (requesting help or accommodations, conferencing, accepting feedback, smoke and mirrors, goal setting schema, pyramid process)

- test preparation (objective test-taking cycle, test-taking critique)

- test taking (triage, splashdown, eliminating options, pair testing)

See the Appendices for specific examples of each strategy.

Matching strategies with the teaching structures (Figure 5.8) can provide the support and education that the diverse learner needs to be successful in a block schedule.

LECTURE

If the dissemination of factual data is the focus of a lesson, the most efficient method of delivering the information remains lecture. Lecture, and the note taking required by lecturing, is often a difficult task for students with learning needs. Successful note taking from a lecture requires students to be proficient in several complex skills, the most important of which are listening comprehension, isolating salient ideas, paraphrasing, and organizing information while spelling and writing. If a student is weak in any one of these skills, his or her notes will be sketchy, incomplete, or inaccurate.

FIGURE 5.8. DOVETAILING STRATEGIES AND TEACHING STRUCTURES

	Reciprocal Teaching	Small Group	Seminar	Concept Attainment	Tutorial	Adaptive Education	Lecture
Attention	✖	✖	✖			✖	
Reading	✖		✖		✖	✖	
Composing				✖	✖	✖	
Computation	✖			✖	✖	✖	
Problem Solving		✖				✖	
Identifying Key Information	✖		✖	✖	✖	✖	✖
Memorizing				✖	✖	✖	
Understanding	✖	✖	✖	✖	✖	✖	✖
Organizing				✖	✖	✖	
Advocating	✖	✖				✖	
Test Taking						✖	

Content teachers who wish to use lecture during the explanation section of the block can plan modifications with the support teachers so that a student's weakness in any one skill does not present a barrier (see Figure 5.9, on pages 98–99). Some of those modifications might be:

- tape-record or videotape the lecture

- provide a looseleaf model as an exemplar for students to compare their notes against

- provide cloze-style notes or open frame notes that students complete from the lecture (see Appendix C for an example of cloze-style notes)

- allow time for note taking partners to compare notes after the lecture (see Appendix C for note taking partner strategy.)

- begin with short lecture periods and lengthen the time as the year proceeds

- provide carbonless copypaper to skillful note takers so they can share their notes with those who are less skilled

- provide students with teacher's lecture notes and have students highlight during lecture
- have the support teacher script on an overhead as the lecture proceeds

FIGURE 5.9. MODIFIED LECTURE PLAN

Structure: Lecture   Subject: American Literature
Strategy: Cornell Notes   Content: Puritanism as the character base
           Guided Notes   of American Literature

Stage	Time	Agenda	What the Content Teacher Does	What the Support Teacher Does
Explanation	10 min	Reinforcement/Feed-back: homework (set up 6 Cornell pages) Objectives/focus: —Advance organizer: guided notes religious freedom egalitarianism Protestantism work ethic piety literature as moral guide —Structure lecture: purpose and use of notes	1. Circulate to record homework—correct errors in Cornell format as students copy guided note headings onto the top of each page 2. Leads question/answer session: —What is difficult for you when taking notes? —How can notes be used after a lecture?	2. Records student responses on chart
	30 min	Explanation/Instruction: Strategy—Cornell notes format Itinerary—content lecture on Puritan ethic and some historical background (follow guided note headings)		Describes steps in Cornell note strategy (See Appendix C for Cornell-style notes)
			Lecture: religious freedom egalitarianism Protestantism work ethic piety literature—moral guide	Prepares a looseleaf model

Stage	Time	Agenda	What the Content Teacher Does	What the Support Teacher Does
Application	20 min	Kid-watching: —Guided practice —Group Work —Corrective feedback —Checking against model —Evaluation for pull out instruction —Monitoring for mastery	1. Assign students to note taking partner pairs (partners compare notes, discuss differences, fill in any missing information from each other's notes) 2. Cue for on task behavior 3. Intervene in discussions to settle disputes 4. Direct pairs to compare both notes against looseleaf model 5. Identify students who will need more detailed guided notes during future lectures	
Synthesis	5 min	Closure: —Homework: read pages 45–46 in anthology, fill in Cornell notes from text, highlight any information that occurs in both text and teacher lecture	1. Assigns homework 2. Restates steps in Cornell note taking process 3. Circulates to answer questions as students begin the text reading, note taking, and highlighting	Adaptive education 1. Photocopies looseleaf model with key words from text omitted to give to students who have demonstrated a need 2. Pulls out students and instructs in use of more detailed guided notes
	25 min	Improving comprehension/memory: —Summarize: steps in Cornell note taking —Begin homework reading, note taking, and highlighting		

6

ASSESSMENT

When the content teacher and the support teacher begin to discuss and share assessment of student progress, the potential for conflict is the greatest. Support teachers are comfortable with and accustomed to individualizing assessment for each student. Content teachers are comfortable with and accustomed to standardizing assessment. Support teachers are comfortable with and accustomed to using ongoing corrective feedback. Content teachers are comfortable with and accustomed to districtwide standardized grading systems. Support teachers are comfortable with providing a variety of testing accommodations to bypass student learning disabilities and weaknesses. Content teachers are comfortable with all students being tested in the same way. Fortunately, both the support teacher and the content teacher want assessments that provide a clear picture of students' knowledge, understanding and growth. It is this common interest, the time provided by block scheduling, and two professionals working cooperatively that can support the development of assessment tools that move well beyond one-dimensional testing. Both professionals must walk a fine line between keeping expectations for performance high but reasonable, without providing so much help that the student is crippled by enabling behavior from adults.

AUTHENTIC ASSESSMENT

Authentic assessment is one type of assessment that works well in the extended times provided by block scheduling and gives an excellent opportunity for students with learning needs to show their knowledge. Authentic assessment also provides valuable opportunities for high achieving students to extend their knowledge. Students have the time to immerse themselves in genuine, real-life learning and skill development. Assessment can become an ongoing, educational process rather than a series of activities that yield discrete products and bits of factual information. Grant Wiggins (1990) characterizes authentic assessment as that which:

♦ Involves tasks that are of value, engage students' interests, and at which students can excel (tasks worth learning and teaching)

- Simulates the challenges facing adults or workers in the field of study (not just isolated demonstration of skills and facts)

- Contains challenges that require knowledge in use (students must use a repertoire of strategies)

- Focuses on the students' abilities to produce a quality product and/ or performance (effectiveness and craftsmanship become more necessary than one right answer)

- Allows for thorough preparation, self-assessment (correction and revision by the students are required)

- Relies on assessor judgment, in reference to clear and appropriate criteria (the quality of responses, products, or performances are judged on preestablished rubrics)

- Requires interactions between assessor and assessee (teachers and students share the responsibility for assessment)

- Focuses on students' abilities to justify answers (students respond to follow-up or probing questions)

- Encourages in-depth, extended responses (students' patterns of thought and habits of the mind are revealed)

- Establishes a pattern of student behavior (consistency over time can be observed)

As these characteristics suggest, authentic assessment pieces are difficult and time consuming to construct. The support teacher and the content teacher can ease the process by planning the assessment pieces together. The use of focusing statements and questions suggested by McTighe (1994) between the content teacher and the support teacher regarding authentic assessment might sound like the following:

Content Teacher: I would like to assess very specific content knowledge.

Support Teacher: I would also like to assess how the students gain that knowledge. What processes for acquiring knowledge were you considering teaching? Let's talk about how they may need to differ for the brightest and the neediest of the students.

Content Teacher: What product or performance will be appropriate for each student and will also provide enough evidence of attainment?

Support Teacher: That can best be answered by providing choice within limits that allows for all students to use their learner strengths in demonstrating what they know. Let's start with the strengths that you have already recognized. How can we capitalize on those strengths?

Content Teacher: Many of my students seem to work together. They are very comfortable in small groups. I want the students to work in cooperative groups in preparation for presenting their product/performance.

Support Teacher: That sounds great. Perhaps I can help set up the groups based on the individual strengths and needs each student has and the prior knowledge they bring. Depending on whether the students themselves work at the evaluative level and set their own criteria, or an outside audience be will involved that will also be helpful to know.

Content Teacher: I want to develop specific indicators for performance.

Support Teacher: That's correct, but you want to be careful that you aren't giving them an oversimplified recipe to follow that requires little thought. These performances need to be rich and multidimensional and not simply fun activities that do not say something directly about a significant outcome, standard, or process.

Content Teacher: How do we create scoring rubrics that don't minimize or reduce the authentic task to the simplest elements?

Support Teacher: We could work together to identify the most critical content and process in your course. We would need to be very specific about the level of student engagement you want. Then careful analysis of the performance outcome within that course will identify the discrete parts that must be included in the scoring rubric.

Content Teacher: I'll provide them with models and exemplars for performance.

Support Teacher: Showing them a range from poor to excellent will also structure their performance. Will you be using this assessment to make summative decisions, formative decisions, or diagnostic decisions?

Content Teacher: I want us to think more about that. Then, depending on what we decide, we'll consider what tools for scoring would be most appropriate.

Support Teacher: Can we get back together to decide....

TRADITIONAL TESTS

Not all content lends itself to authentic assessment. If the memorization of discrete bits of information is the curricular goal, the content will not be rigorous enough to require authentic assessment. Standardized, teacher-made tests of curricular information requiring recognition, recall, and production of short answers and essays may still be necessary. This type of test is limited in that it is static and does not measure a student's understanding of information nor is it engaging enough to keep all students motivated. The grade on a standardized, teacher-made test simply measures the student's ability to recognize or recall discrete bits of information on one particular day.

A variety of test modifications and techniques can be used to adapt teacher-made tests so that all students may compete equally. Well-constructed traditional tests should reflect closely what and how the content was taught. The terminology used in class and in the text should be used on the test. If the primary instruction was through discussion and problem solving, the test should be in essay format. If lecture and textbook reading were the primary method of disseminating information, the test should be matching, multiple choice, and fill-in-the-blank. Finally, the number of questions on a traditional test should be related to the amount of class time spent on the items.

Following a few simple guidelines for the format of the teacher-made tests will increase the opportunity for all students to do well on the test (Salend 1995):

- tests should cover only the most relevant and necessary information
- tests should be clearly printed on nondistracting background using 12- to 18-point print
- tests should reflect the style students are used to reading
- tests should be sequenced to ease the transition from item to item
- tests should be prepared with white space clearly separating items
- fonts with serifs should be used for tests with large amounts of text

- fonts without serifs should be used to focus the student's attention on titles or directions

- frequent tests or quizzes should be given rather than just unit exams

Even if a test has been constructed with extreme care, many students with learning needs will require testing accommodations. Many simple and easy-to-administer modifications made during the administration of a teacher-made test can allow students to demonstrate competence more accurately. These accommodations are easy to provide and can be used in any setting. Support teachers are familiar with these accommodations and can help students and the content teacher in the use of the accommodation during tests. Some of the most common and successful accommodations are:

- students write answers directly on the test

- students read the test aloud to a listener, reading errors are corrected

- students use learning aides (calculators, computers with spell checkers, etc.)

- students use extensions of time for the completion of the test

- students use referenced notes or graphic organizers they have created

- teachers record answers as student takes test

- teachers scribe the student's oral essay

- teachers read questions aloud to the student

- teachers highlight key words and phrases

- teachers teach test-taking skills during the test

- teachers give feedback on time, strategies, progress

- teachers clarify, paraphrase, or simplify directions and questions

- teachers reduce multiple choice options

It is important to note that these test accommodations (see Figure 6.1) should be instituted only when there is clear, objective evidence of need. Accommodations should not be used to replace the need for students to spend adequate time and energy on preparation and the cooperating teachers who administer these accommodations must be careful to avoid helping students to the point of cheating. Because of these accommodations, issues of fairness sometimes arise. It is important to communicate to students, teachers, and

FIGURE 6.1. CURRICULAR AND TEST ACCOMMODATIONS CHECKLIST

Student: Bill Hodges				Adaptation/Accommodation	Year: 1997–98			
Subjects					Report Period			
Eng.	Math	Health	Art I		1	2	3	4
✔		✔		Grade was based on only the most critical information of the course	✔	✔	✔	✔
✔			✔	Quantity of required work, compared to other students, was reduced	✔	✔	✔	✔
✔	✔	✔		Special provisions for tests and quizzes were made:	✔	✔	✔	✔
				Tests were read to the student				
	✔	✔		Extended time to complete tests was given	✔	✔	✔	✔
✔		✔		Cued notes, graphic organizers, or referenced notes were used	✔	✔	✔	✔
				Test questions were explained and/or discussed in detail				
✔		✔		Tests were specially designed to match assignment modifications	✔	✔	✔	✔
✔	✔			Assignments were modified:	✔	✔	✔	✔
✔				Oral answers were accepted in the place of some written work	✔	✔	✔	✔
	✔		✔	Fewer questions, problems, essays, projects were required	✔	✔	✔	✔

Teacher's Signature and Comments:

Joanne Eisenberger, 10th English:
    Bill will still need to make a constant effort to do well

Robert Bertrando, Geometry:
    Bill must do all the homework to be prepared for the tests

Marcia Conti-D'Antonio, Learning Support:
    I will be monitoring Bill's use of these accommodations and reporting to you

Fred Strange, Art:
    I will expect the quality of Bill's portfolio to be high

Karen Brown, Health:
    Bill should be very successful with these accommodations

parents that fair does not mean identical. Fair means that every student receives what he or she needs to learn and to demonstrate that knowledge. These accommodations should be clearly reported to parents. Report cards can be coded or a simple checklist can be used. (For additional formats to use when reporting to parents, see Appendix J.)

ASSESSMENT THROUGH OBSERVATION: KID-WATCHING

The application segment of the block provides the best opportunity to observe students, interact with students, document student achievement, and interpret student learning (Goodman, 1997). Students' growth in the use of strategies, their ability to use higher-order thinking skills, their mastery of the content, and the need for pull-out adaptive or tutorial education can be determined. This should be a very active time for both cooperating teachers because this is the best time for true assessment. This is the best place in the block to figure out what the students have learned, how the learning has occurred and why the learning of some students is delayed. Observations, interactive and probing questions, and checklists (Figure 6.2) can be used to identify the need for whole-class instruction in specific strategies. The need for pull-out instruction can also be made by identifying a discrepancy between a specific student or a small group of students and the performance of the other students within the same classroom. These students can then be taken aside for specific instruction in strategies that match the students' learning style or that bypass the students' weaknesses and support their strengths. This diagnostic teaching approach, called dipsticking, places a strong emphasis on how students are learning and on the strategies that make the learning experience successful for the student. Less emphasis is placed on the end product of learning as the only assessment.

Diagnostic teaching, or kid watching, has several benefits for students with learning needs. First, the teachers can continually assess students in an authentic setting as the students use the strategies and content. This allows the cooperating teachers to shift away from materials and tasks as the only method of assessment. Second, student progress can be tracked over time, in a variety of settings, and at various points in time. This allows the cooperating teachers to look carefully at students' learning efficiency not just their abilities. Finally, the picture that emerges from this diagnostic, dynamic approach is a more accurate picture of the students' mastery of the course work than any static test can show.

Good classroom management during kid watching is essential. Both the support teacher and the content teacher need to remain acutely aware of what is happening in all parts of the classroom at all times, intervening promptly with suggestions and cues. Both teachers need to respond to individuals while keeping the group as a whole on task. These two behaviors, called "withitness" and

FIGURE 6.2. SKILL EVALUATION CHECKLIST

Skill Evaluation Checklist

Date _____

Teacher _____

requests instruction when work is difficult	uses suggestions given by teacher	quiets self, or allows the teacher to quiet	accepts feedback from teachers, peers	has a variety of strategies to choose from	chooses strategies that match problem	learns new strategies	works toward achieving goal	Students
M	M	M	G	G	G	G	G	Barry White
Y	G	G	G	W	Y	W	W	John Carnes
G	G	G	G	G	G	W	G	Barbara Smith

M = Mastered	Student does this automatically. This is part of the student's school habits. No one has to remind the student to do this.
G = Good	Student can do this but sometimes needs to be reminded. Not an automatic part of this student's behavior.
W = Needs Work	Student knows how to do this but almost always needs someone to remind him or her.
Y = Not Yet	Student cannot do this or refuses to do this.

"overlapping" by Kounin (1970) are crucial to maintaining and sustaining student attention to tasks.

The support teacher and the content teacher need to decide together which student characteristics they will look for during the kid watching segment (see Figure 6.3). Once identified, these behaviors will provide a unifying framework for instruction. The support teacher and the content teacher can cue students in the use of these behaviors, reinforce the students' use of these behaviors, and monitor the students' need for tutorial instruction or mastery of these behaviors. One such list was suggested by Feuerstein (1980).

The application segment of the block is an excellent time to teach students to be reflective and to share in the assessment tasks. Asking the students to help create the rubrics for projects, essays, discussions, and their own skill development is one way to involve them in the process. Having students evaluate themselves through behavior checklists (Figure 6.4) followed by interviews and conferences is another.

FIGURE 6.3. CHARACTERISTICS OF HIGHER- LEVEL THINKING

CHARACTERISTIC	DESCRIPTION	BEHAVIOR	CUES/PROMPTS
Perseverance	Working until solution is reached	Tries again, debates strategy, changes strategies	Look at this again. What else might you try?
Decreased impulsivity	Pausing to reflect or clarify, requesting more information	Asks for facts, pauses before answering	Speed doesn't count. Gather your thoughts. Take your time.
Flexibility	Considering other points of view, trying new approaches	Paraphrases others, accepts suggestions or directions, evaluates responses	Can anyone think of another way to....Let's try looking at this another way.
Metacognition	Analyzing, describing one's own thought processes	Retraces steps, describes strategies and processes used	Go through the steps aloud. How did you do that?
Careful review	Proofing work, comparing work to criteria or exemplar	Reflects on accuracy of work; checks to insure accuracy	Did you compare your work to the rubric? Have you used a peer editor?
Problem posing	Asking questions and finding problems to solve	Wonders. Asks for proof or evidence	How do you know? What would happen if...?
Past knowledge	Using prior knowledge or past learning	Makes connection to past experience, content or ideas	Does this remind you of anything else? Where else might this be useful?
Enjoyment of problem solving	Solving problems with increasing joy and independence	Comments positively. On task for extended period of time.	You're doing great. Keep working. I'm pleased to see you're hanging in there.
Precise language	Using appropriate descriptive words and labels	Uses analogies, complete sentences. Concise.	Stop and think first. What is the scientific word for that?

FIGURE 6.4. SKILLS CHECKLIST

Teacher					Student			
✔ mas-tered	✔ good	✔ needs work	✔ not yet	**SKILL**	✔ mas-tered	✔ good	✔ needs work	✔ not yet
				Keeping Track				
				homework recorded in as-signment book				
				project deadlines planned out until due date				
				test preparation times planned out each night				
				materials needed in school and well organized				
				grades are recorded in as-signment book				
				Self-Assigned Homework				
				asks for editing on writing; corrects before due				
				prepares projects beyond re-quirements				
				practices math without being assigned				
				uses a test prep. routine to memorize information				
				Self-Determination				
				asks for accommodations				
				knows and works according to learning style				
				prioritizes work				
				works toward achieving the goals set				

✔ mas-tered	✔ good	✔ needs work	✔ not yet	SKILL	✔ mas-tered	✔ good	✔ needs work	✔ not yet
				Time Management				
				does test preparation in addition to homework				
				completes homework on time				
				on time to classes				
				to school on time with strong attendance				
				Other?				

Mastered	I do this automatically. This is part of my school habits. No one has to remind me to do this.
Good	Even though I know this will help me be more successful, I sometimes need to be reminded to do this.
Needs Work	I know how to do this but I almost always need someone to remind me.
Not Yet	I refuse to do this. I don't think this is necessary for me.

PLANNING FOR ASSESSMENT

Establishing clear criteria for performance, creating an environment that supports self-evaluation and a sense of community, and teaching students to establish rubrics that make distinctions between acceptable and unacceptable performance are difficult enough. When including students with learning needs in the equation, careful planning is critical. The cooperating teachers need to agree on the type of assessment that will be used and who will be responsible for observing, recording, and administering the assessments. The application portion of the block (Figure 6.5) can be structured to take maximum advantage of having two teachers in a classroom.

FIGURE 6.5. APPLICATION SEGMENT OF A BLOCK

Stage	Time	Agenda	What the Content Teacher Does	What the Support Teacher Does
Application	30 min	Kid Watching: —Guided practice —Group work —Corrective feedback —Checking against expert —Checking against exemplar —Evaluation for pull-out —Monitoring for mastery —Teaching for transfer	1. Provides assessment for different learning styles 2. Documents the performance of students	1. Provides assessment accommodations for learning weaknesses and disabilities 2. Documents the performance of students with learning needs
			1. Observe and record student use of strategies, skills, habits, knowledge 2. Observe and judge student products and performance according to an established rubric 3. Focus on the students' justifications, strategies and/or self-corrections 4. Insure that adequate time and resources are available to all students 5. Administer cooperatively designed assessments 6. Intervene promptly and accurately when inappropriate behavior occurs 7. Restore inattentive student to the tasks without interrupting the lesson	

Content teachers and support teachers who wish to work cooperatively during assessment will find it beneficial to learn more about:

♦ performance criteria

♦ rubric creation

♦ task analysis

♦ performance assessment grading

♦ complex thinking and learning measurement

- communication of student performance (See Appendix J for parent communication memo, student liaison report and monthly planning log)

- self-advocacy (see Appendix H for grade tracking)

APPENDIX A

GOAL SETTING

GOAL SETTING SCHEMA

Students need to be taught to clarify their intentions. Making broad general statements such as, "I want to do better," or, "I will try harder," permits self-deception. Goal setting schemas or routines can instruct students in how to make their intentions concrete, small, and achievable. Nothing builds success like success. Students can experience success by choosing and declaring their intentions with care and by setting goals that are challenging but possible. Effective goals, the kinds that actually motivate, have these characteristics:

- They are concrete and specific. The goal is phrased clearly.

- They are realistic. The goal is challenging but not beyond the bounds of what is reasonable.

- They are measurable. Everyone can tell if the goal has been achieved.

- They include a time frame for achievement.

- They are anchored in a person's personal values.

- They are written and published. An unrecorded goal is only a wish and not as likely to be achieved.

- They are achievable without overreliance on someone else.

- They identify a reward.

SCHEMA 1—SMOKE AND MIRRORS

The purpose of the smoke and mirrors strategy is to teach students a way to make goals concrete. Students often believe they have committed to goals by thinking about them. If a goal is not affirmed, it is usually not a goal but a wish. Wishes occasionally come true but not as often as goals. The process of writing down goals and making them public through an affirmation process dissipates the smoke and provides a mirror through which students can reflect on their progress.

1. Self-Questioning

> What are some good things that might happen to me if I improve my school performance?

> What are some bad things that might happen to me if I improve my school performance?

> What could keep me from improving my school performance?

> Who can help me improve my school performance?

2. Goal Setting (Follow the eight characteristics of effective goals under goal setting schema)

> a. As a short-term goal, I will _____.

> b. As a mid-term goal, I will _____.

> c. As a long-term goal, I will _____.

3. Affirmation

> Share your goals with someone you identified as helping you to improve.

> Explain how you will achieve your goals and what the reward will be.

> Arrange to meet regularly with the person to discuss your progress.

4. Reflection (Think about these things after the meeting with your support person)

> Were you satisfied with your progress?

> Were your goals clear and sharp in your mind?

> Did the support person you used keep you focused and honest?

SCHEMA 2—PYRAMID PROCESS

The purpose of the pyramid process is to teach students a goal setting schema or routine that breaks difficult goals into small achievable stages. The achievement of the primary (long-term) goal is expressed as a series of smaller goals and spread over a lengthy period. The goals should dovetail from one level of the pyramid to the next. Students may prepare the pyramid from bottom to top or top to bottom.

One long-term
goal: achievable by
the end of this school term

1. _____

Two midterm goals: achievable
by the end of the current semester

1. _____

2._____

Three short-term goals: achievable
by the end of the current marking period

1. _____

2. _____

3. _____

1. These goals are important to me because _____.

2. My reward for achieving these goals will be _____.

APPENDIX B

LEVELS OF QUESTIONS

Evaluation—*Development of opinions, judgments, or decisions with respect to criteria; the criteria must be identified.*

Do you agree _____?

What do you think about _____?

What is the most important _____?

Prioritize _____?

How would you decide about _____?

What criteria would you use to assess _____?

Synthesis—*Combination of ideas to form a new whole.*

What would you prefer/infer from _____?

What ideas can you add to _____?

How would you create/design a new _____?

What might happen if you combine _____ with _____?

What solutions would you suggest for _____?

Analysis—*Separation of a whole into component parts.*

What are the parts/features of _____?

Classify _____ according to _____.

Outline/diagram/web _____.

How does _____ compare/contrast to _____?

Application—*Use facts, rules, principles.*

How is _____ an example of _____?

How is _____ related to _____?

Why is _____ significant?

Comprehension—*Organization and selection of facts and ideas.*

Retell _____ in your own words.

What is the main idea of _____?

Knowledge—*Identification and recall of information.*

Who, what, when, where, how _____?

Describe _____.

APPENDIX C

IDENTIFYING KEY INFORMATION

Students need to be taught strategies for identifying key information as an essential skill for academic success. Written notes, either from the text as it is read or from a class lecture, are both a record of what has been presented and of what material for which the student is responsible.

POST-IT PROCESS

The purpose of the Post-It process is to teach the students a way to have main ideas, questions, examples, information, and supporting details readily accessible and near the appropriate passages of a school text. It is a concrete way for students to interact with a text without defacing the property.

- ◆ Steps
  - Read text silently or subvocally.
  - On a Post-It, paraphrase the main idea, definition, steps in a process, supporting detail, or a question that needs to be clarified or explained.
  - Place the Post-It in the text, slightly off the page, to serve as a place marker.
  - Use the Post-It during class discussion or guided practice, while completing assignments or preparing for tests, or to remind you to ask for clarification of information.
  - Add details from class discussions, lectures, and handouts, or prepare additional Post-Its.
  - Peel the Post-Its off the text and use them in conjunction with an appropriate memorization strategy when preparing for a test.

CORNELL NOTES

The purpose of the Cornell method of note taking is to provide the student with a method of recording information that is self-organized and concise. The Cornell method allows the student to produce a polished set of notes that is both a record of the material assigned and a study and review guide.

- ◆ Steps
  - Name and date the top of the page.
  - Draw a line three inches from the left edge of the paper. (The page is divided into a one-third and a two-thirds segment.) Label the one-third column RECALL.
  - Write notes in the two-thirds segment of the page. Take brief notes using key words. Skip lines between main ideas. Leave spaces if an idea is missed or questions arise.
  - As soon as possible after class, read through the notes and fill in any blanks. Highlight the key words and ideas.
  - Fill in the RECALL column with key words, mnemonic devices, diagrams, or questions.
  - Draw a line across the paper one or two inches from the bottom and label this SUMMARY. Write a brief summary of the notes on this page in your own words.

Ocean Facts	10/15/97
RECALL	KEY INFORMATION
P I—AAA	5 oceans—**Pacific, Indian, Atlantic, Antarctic, Arctic**
Deepest?	Deepest—Atlantic
Largest?	

SUMMARY

Five oceans cover the earth. They are the Pacific, the Atlantic,...

  - Review the notes daily by folding the page so that only the RECALL column is showing.

NOTE-TAKING PARTNER

The purpose of the note-taking partner process is to instruct the student in a strategy for filling in incomplete class lecture notes. This strategy is particularly well suited for strong auditory learners who are focused on retaining information and for students who have spelling and writing fluency difficulty. This strategy is also helpful for students with poor auditory receptive language.

- ◆ Steps
  - Two students take notes during a lecture.
  - The two students then compare and contrast their notes with their partner's notes and fill in any missing information. Notes can be taken on pressure-sensitive paper, each person's notes can be photocopied, or the students can sit together with their individual notes following the lecture.

SKIMMING

The purpose of skimming is to provide students with a system for rapid reading of critical information. Students are taught to scan text for key words and main ideas.

- ◆ Steps
  - Read the question you are answering and identify a key word.
  - Quickly move from line to line in the text, looking for the key word.
  - Stop when you find the key word and read slowly.
  - Read the question again.
  - Ask, "Can I answer the question now?"
  - Write the answer.

GUIDED NOTES

The purpose of guided notes (also called cloze notes or note-taking frames) is to provide the student who is not able to listen, write, or identify key information rapidly an intermediate step in the note-taking process.

♦ Steps

- The teacher provides the student with the two-thirds segment of Cornell notes with the key information omitted. The notes follow the teacher's lecture or the text reading.

- Listen (or read) and fill in the key words or ideas.

- As soon as possible after class, read through the notes and fill in any blanks. Highlight the key words and ideas.

- Fill in the RECALL column with key words, mnemonic devices, diagrams, or questions.

- Draw a line across the paper one or two inches from the bottom and label this SUMMARY. Write a brief summary of the notes on this page in your own words.

- Review the notes daily by folding the page so that only the RECALL column is showing.

Example:

RECALL	Ocean Facts 10/15/97
	_____ oceans: P ____, A ____, I ____, A ____, A ____
	Deepest: _____

THREE-COLUMN NOTE TAKING

The purpose of three-column note taking is to provide the student with a concrete aid for transfer and organization of information and rules when working independently.

♦ Steps

- Divide a page into three columns as follows:

Problem (or Vocabulary word)	Rule	Example

- Complete the information needed in each column and use the notes as an exemplar when doing independent work.

PREDICTING TEST QUESTIONS

The purpose of predicting test questions is for the student to prepare for tests from the day the material is introduced. The student divides a page into three columns—main ideas (answer), critical information (question), and the rationale they used for picking the ideas and information. The list that the student generates is used for rehearsal and retrieval practice and as part of a debriefing process after the test.

- ◆ Steps

  - Label a section of a notebook TEST QUESTIONS. Divide the page into three columns as follows:

Test Questions for the Battles of the Civil War 12/9/97		
Main Idea	Critical Information	Rationale
Lincoln	Who made a speech after the Battle of Gettysburg?	Mr. C. said it three times today.
Antietam	What is the most famous Civil War battle fought in Maryland?	Book & Mr. C. talked about this
Sherman	Which Union general ordered the burning of Atlanta?	End of chapter questions & notes

  - After each lecture, reading assignment, or homework assignment add several questions to list.

  - Confirm the information with a study partner or the instructor.

  - Use the list with a rehearsal and retrieval strategy that matches your learning style.

  - After taking the test, compare your list with the test to see if your information was complete.

PERSONAL CHECKLIST

The purpose of a personalized checklist is to provide the student with a systematic method of checking his or her work. These checklists are especially good for students who repeatedly make the same errors.

- ◆ Steps

  - The student, with the guidance of the teacher, identifies typical errors that he or she makes and forgets to check.

- The checklist is typed up on a bookmark and placed in the text to use while doing homework or taking a test.

Example:

> ### Math Checklist
>
> 1. Did I copy the problem correctly?
> 2. Did I highlight the signs?
> 3. Did I record my splashdown?
> 4. Did I add when I should multiply?
> 5. Did I label my answer?
> 6. Did I answer the question?
> 7. Is my answer near my estimate?
> 8. Did I follow the order of operations?

APPENDIX D

UNDERSTANDING INFORMATION

GRAPHIC ORGANIZERS

The purpose of using graphic organizers is to provide the student with a structure that organizes large amounts of information or abstract information into a graphic representation. A student can then use the information on the graphic organizer to prepare for tests, write essays, correct understanding, analyze information, draw conclusions, and so forth.

♦ Steps

- The student selects an appropriate "blank" from an assortment provided by the instructor or creates a mind map using circles and connected lines.

- The student gathers information and places the information onto the graphic organizer in appropriate boxes, columns, circles, etc.

- The student can use the graphic organizer to prepare for tests, write essays, correct understanding, analyze information, draw conclusions, prepare a lab report.

GOWIN'S VEE GRAPHIC ORGANIZER

The purpose of Gowin's Vee is to provide a structure for students to scaffold information. It is accompanied by a scoring rubric that establishes the expectation for more authentic work and higher-level thinking. Students use Gowin's Vee as a graphic organizer to scaffold information as a way to make abstractions concrete.

Students complete the left side and center of this scaffolding device after the pre-lab reading. The right side of the Vee is completed by the students during and after the lab, when they are able to answer the Focus Questions and the New Focus Questions.

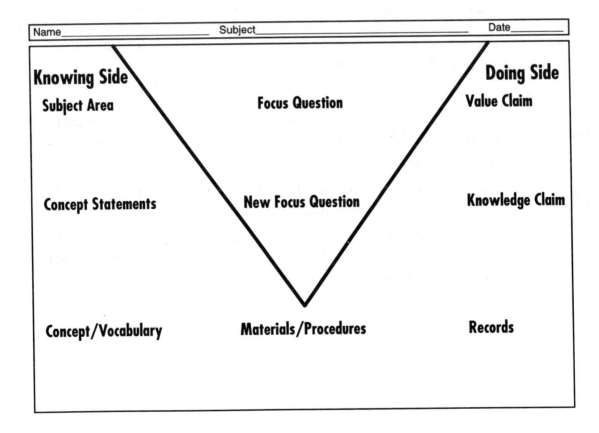

From *Biology: Principles and Explorations* (pp. 28–30), by G. B. Johnson and P. H. Raven, 1996, New York: Holt, Rinehart and Winston. Copyright 1996 by Holt, Rinehart and Winston. Adapted with permission.

Evaluating Vee Reports

Evaluate your student's constructed Vee reports by scoring them according to the criteria shown in the Vee on the following page:

Knowing Side

Concept Statements

0 No concepts are identified.
1 A few concepts are identified, and no concepts statements or a concept written is really the knowledge claim sought in the laboratory exercise.
2 Concepts and at least one type of concept statement are identified.
3 Concepts and two types of concept statements are identified.
4 Concepts, two types of concept statements, and all relevant vocabulary are identified.

Doing Side

Value Claim

0 No value claim is given.
1 A claim consistent with the significance of the investigation describes the usefulness of the knowledge for pure or applied scientific endeavors.

Focus Question

0 No question is identified.
1 A question is identified, but does not focus upon the objectives and the major event or the conceptual side of the vee.
2 A focus question is identified; includes concepts, but does not suggest materials or procedure, or the wrong materials and procedures are identified in relation to the rest of the laboratory exercise.
3 A clear focus question is identified; includes concepts to be used and suggests the procedure and materials.

Knowledge Claim

0 No knowledge claim is identified.
1 A knowledge claim is unrelated to the knowing side.
2 A knowledge claim includes a concept that is using improper context, or any generalization that is inconsistent with record.
3 A knowledge claim includes the concepts from the focus question and is derived from the records.
4 Same as above, but the knowledge claim leads to focus question

New Focus Question

0 No new focus question is given.
1 A new focus question consistent with the knowledge claim is identified.

Records

0 No records or observations are identified.
1 Recordsare identified but are inconsistent with focus question or the major event.
2 Records or observations are identified but not both.
3 Records are identified for the major event; but observations are inconsistent with the intent of the focus question.
4 Records are identified for the major event and observations are consistent with the focus question and grade level and ability of the student.

Materials/Procedures

0 No materials
1 The materials and procedure are identified, but are inconsistent with the focus question.
2 The materials and procedure are identified, and are consistent with the focus question.
3 Same as above, but also suggests what records will be taken.

FIVE PARAGRAPH ESSAY GRAPHIC ORGANIZER

Big Ideas

What is this whole idea about?

Main Idea:	Main Idea:	Main Idea:	

Supporting Points

What is important to understand about this?

So What?

From "An Instrumental Model for Teaching Learning Strategies," by E. S. Ellis, 1991, *Focus on Exceptional Children, 23,* pp. 1–24. Copyright 1991. Reprinted with permission.

DEBATE ORGANIZER GRAPHIC ORGANIZER

OUR OVERALL POSITION:

	What we will say:	Other side's likely position:	How we'll respond:
Big Idea			

Supporting Points			

	If…	If…	If…
Reasoning	Then…	Then…	Then…

From "An Instrumental Model for Teaching Learning Strategies," by E. S. Ellis, 1991, *Focus on Exceptional Children, 23,* pp. 1–24. Copyright 1991. Reprinted with permission.

COURT CASE ANALYSIS GRAPHIC ORGANIZER

What are they arguing about?	
Party 1:	Party 2:
Position:	Position:
Facts of the Case	Facts of the Case
If...	If...
Then...	Then...
Your Position:	
Personal Connection:	

From "An Instrumental Model for Teaching Learning Strategies," by E. S. Ellis, 1991, *Focus on Exceptional Children, 23*, pp. 1–24. Copyright 1991. Reprinted with permission.

MATH ASSAULT

The purpose of the math assault strategy is to give a student a systematic process for solving high-level mathematics problems using both auditory and visual modes. This strategy allows an instructor to detect and correct errors in a student's mathematical problem solving process and ends with a "paper memory" that a student can use in solving other abstract mathematical problems. Color coding paper to organize topics and/or laminating the model sheets for permanent storage is also useful.

- ◆ Steps

  - Write a problem on the top of a notebook page or 6" x 8" note card.

  - Verbalize and record the mathematical steps as you solve the problem.

  - Verbalize the steps again as you write the steps in sentence form beside each step.

  - Use the paper or card for reference when solving similar problems and when preparing for tests and quizzes, or as a cued note system during a test.

Factor completely $x^2 - 8x + 15$ and check using FOIL	
1. (x)(x)	1. x times itself is x^2 so I can write that in each parenthesis.
2. (x –)(x –)	2. The plus sign in front of the 15 tells me both signs will be the same. The minus sign in front of the 8x tells me both signs will be negative. I can write that in each parenthesis.
3. (x – 3)(x – 5)	3. What two numerals will multiply to the last numeral and add or subtract to the middle numeral? 1, 3, 5, and 15 are the multiples. 3 and 5 add to 8 and multiply to 15; I can write 3 and 5 in the parenthesis.
4. FOIL	4. Write the FOIL (First, Outside, Inside, Last) mnemonic under my solution.
5. x^2	5. The first two terms in each parenthesis means x times x. That is x^2.
6. –5x	6. The outside terms in each parenthesis is x times -5. That is -5x.
7. –3x	7. The inside terms are -3 times x. That is –3x.
8. +15	8. The last terms are –3 times –5. That is +15.
9. –5x and –3x are –8x	9. The only like terms are the middle two. –5x –3x combine to –8x.
10. $x^2 - 8x + 15$	10. Write the complete expression and compare to the original problem

APPENDIX E

SUSTAINING ATTENTION AND CONCENTRATION

CONSTRUCTING AND USING AN ATTENTION TAPE

The purpose of the attention tape process is to provide the student with a method of monitoring and charting his or her attention while performing a task that requires interacting with a text, such as reading for understanding. This process is also useful with a student who has an attention deficit disorder when he or she is doing any task that requires sustained attention and is not intrinsically motivating.

- ◆ Steps

  - Make a tape recording that is completely silent except for a pleasant, nonabrasive sound at odd intervals. The recommended time intervals for a 30-minute tape are 3, 4, 3, 5, 4, 2, 4, 3, and 2 minutes.

  - The student is instructed to begin work as the tape begins.

  - Each time the student hears the sound, he or she asks, "Am I on task?" and records a yes or no on a simple score sheet and then returns to the task.

  - At the end of the study period (no more than 30 minutes) the student totals the time he or she was on task. During following study times, the student attempts to improve the on task behavior.

TURTLE FOR SELF-CONTROL

The purpose of the turtle process is to instruct the student in a strategy to use when he or she is about to behave inappropriately in order to teach him or her how to avoid that behavior. This strategy may need to be used in conjunction with strategies on relaxation techniques and a reward system to be most effective. This strategy works well for a student with Attention Deficit Hyperactive

Disorder (ADHD) who feels compelled to move around the classroom at inappropriate times or for a student who tends to be inappropriately aggressive.

- ◆ Steps
  - Tune-in to what is going on in your body when it gets tense, hot, or fidgety.
  - Sit down and mentally draw in your arms and legs like a turtle into its shell.
  - Take several slow deep breaths or tense and release your fists or toes several times.
  - Think about what is the most appropriate behavior. Observe what others are doing.
  - Tune-in to your body again.
  - Return to work.

APPENDIX F

WHAT TO DO BEFORE AND AFTER THE TEST

TEST PREPARATION ROUTINES

Test preparation routines are patterns of behavior that can be taught to students as standard test preparation steps. These routines allow students to narrow their focus and become more productive during study periods. The routines guide students in the use of distributed practice instead of massed practice. Using distributed practice improves student retention and helps demonstrate the disadvantages of cramming. These routines provide an efficient framework for preparation and study of information. Any one of the following routines, once learned by students, will improve test performance.

These routines work best if students combine them with time management planning. Teachers should announce tests far enough in advance for students to complete all the steps in a study routine. Students should record the test in their assignment notebook or calendar, noting the date the test is to be given. Students should then plan back from that date and schedule the steps for the routine they are using. Students who spend sufficient time on their initial study of material will need less review time just before the test. Those students who claim to be unable to remember information unless they cram the night before have inadequate rehearsal and retrieval strategies and are relying on short-term memory. Review is most helpful if it builds on a base of effective initial processing.

OBJECTIVE TEST-TAKING CYCLE

♦ Set a Goal: target a grade that is achievable and manageable

   establish a time frame and plan backward from the test date

   commit to a series of strategies that match your learning style

♦ Identify the key information with a highlighting strategy

- Organize the information with a chunking strategy

- Memorize the information with a rehearsal strategy

- Do a memory check with a retrieval strategy

- Adjust target grade based on the results of the memory check step

- Repeat the third through fifth steps (if time allows) for the information that could not be retrieved

- Take the test using test taking strategies

- Critique test performance using a debriefing strategy

- Repeat the cycle

TEST-TAKING CRITIQUE

The purpose of the test-taking critique is to teach the student a way to reflect on the study routine used for test preparation, to identify the obstacles or causes of poor performance, and to plan to correct those negatives. After a test has been returned, a student completes a simple self-analysis, draws some conclusions about his or her performance, and makes a plan to correct any negative study habits.

- Circle or highlight the items that are true about your preparation for the test that has just been returned to you.

I should have started to prepare sooner than I did.	I started to prepare at least 5 days before the test.
I did not schedule enough time for preparations.	I scheduled the correct amount of time for preparation.
I did the teacher-assigned homework and thought that would be enough.	I assigned additional work to myself so I could be as prepared as possible.
I should have prepared a splashdown.	I prepared a splashdown and used it on the test.
I should have used a different rehearsal strategy.	I used a rehearsal strategy that matched my learning style.
I did not check to see what was in my memory.	I practiced retrieving information from my memory.
I prepared for recognition and I needed recall.	I prepared for both recognition and recall.
I was overconfident.	I knew I was well-prepared and over-learned the material.

I studied the wrong information.	The information I studied was correct and complete because I asked the teacher.
I had trouble understanding the questions or instructions.	I asked for help when I was not sure of the questions or instructions.
I had trouble with the way the test looked.	I asked for help when the way the test was set up got in the way.
I made careless mistakes.	I checked my test for accuracy before handing it in.
I ran out of time.	I requested extended time before beginning the test.
I had to guess too much.	I knew most of the answers and used eliminating options when I did not.
I choked or " blanked out" during the test.	I used a strategy to calm myself when I felt nervous.
I was unfamiliar with parts of the test.	None of the questions on the test was a surprise.
I remember seeing the information but could not pull it out of my memory.	I had practice retrieving the information and could pull it out of my memory.
I misinterpreted what some of the questions were asking.	I made sure I understood the questions before I tried to answer.
Other:	Other:

- ♦ Reflect on what the critique is telling you about your test preparations.

  What did you do well during your preparation?

  What did you do poorly during your preparation?

  Draw some conclusions about your test preparation.

- ♦ Plan a solution for each item that you circled in the left column so you can improve your test scores.

APPENDIX G

MEMORIZING

KEY WORD PICTURES

This rehearsal strategy uses substitution, imagery, association, and humor to remember information. It is used when a large amount of information needs to be retained or when a concept or fact cannot be easily pictured or associated with prior knowledge. This strategy has the added benefit of being appropriate for any style of learner. Visual learners can make the images bold and colorful, auditory learners can include sounds, and kinesthetic learners can include movement.

- ◆ Steps
  - Select a word that has no meaning for you or that you are having trouble retaining.
  - Associate the sound of the word or the look of the word with a vivid, silly, or strange image that is linked to the unknown word.
  - Practice using the image to recall the true meaning of the word or to recognize the true meaning of the word on a test.

- ◆ Examples

  To remember that John Kay invented the Flying Shuttle, picture a giant, white "K" with huge angle wings flying through the blue sky.

  To remember that a crab belongs to the crustacean family, picture a crab holding a huge crust of bread in its claw as it walks down the beach.

  To remember that "roja" is red in Spanish, picture a huge red rose laughing, "Ha, Ha."

- ◆ Guidelines
  - Make the image large and exaggerated.
  - Make the image move, speak, or sing.
  - Make the image bizarre, silly, and unusual.
  - Make the image resonate with sounds like the word to be remembered.

APPENDIX H

SELF-ADVOCACY AND SELF-DETERMINATION STRATEGIES

CONFERENCING

The purpose of the conferencing strategy is to provide the student with the skills to interact cooperatively with teachers, parents, and peers. Learning this process allows the student to gain and share information. Once learned, this strategy can be used to reinforce skills, to gain feedback on progress, to externalize thought processes, and to increase understanding. Conferencing can serve as a catalyst for the creation of new ideas as well as encourage reflection and revision.

♦ Steps

- Determine the purpose of the conference (discussion, problem solving, training, tell-back, feedback, progress report, etc.).

- Listen carefully. Take notes, nod your head, or say "mm-hmm" so the others in the conference know that you are listening.

- Ask questions about anything that you do not understand. Do not argue or insist on your own way.

- Use I messages that are empty of personal criticism. Offer your ideas, opinions, suggestions, etc. Do not argue or insist on your own way.

- Decide which ideas, information, and suggestions you can use and let the other person know.

- Keep a record of the conference.

ACCEPTING FEEDBACK

The purpose of the accepting feedback process is to provide the student with a strategy that enhances the ability to listen to feedback, both positive and negative, and to use that information to change or maintain behavior.

◆ Steps

- Listen carefully while you are receiving the feedback. Take notes, or nod your head, or say "mm-hmm" so that the person giving the feedback knows you are listening.

- Ask questions about anything you don't understand so the feedback is specific and clear. Do not argue with the feedback or try to defend and explain away the feedback.

- Accept the positive feedback and acknowledge the compliment.

- Repeat the suggestions on how to change the negative feedback to positive.

- Decide what you think about the negative feedback by separating your ideas from the other person's ideas and say your ideas aloud.

- Decide if you can follow the suggestions and let the other person know your decision.

- Do what has been decided.

REQUESTING HELP OR ACCOMMODATION

The purpose of the requesting help process is to instruct the student in a strategy that allows the student to seek assistance from others to cope with information, directions, assignments, and personal problems. The same basic steps can be used to teach a student to request his or her accommodations.

◆ Steps

- Decide specifically what the problem is (or what accommodation will be requested) and form it into a statement. Explain who or what is causing the problem, why the accommodation is needed, as well as the effect the problem (accommodation) has.

- Decide if you want help for the problem (accommodation) or if you can solve the problem (ask for the accommodation) alone. (Helps a student to separate power plays, attention-seeking behaviors, and inappropriate accommodation requests from requests for solutions.

If the student's goal is to engage in a battle, help is inappropriate. Words like win or lose, right and wrong, and fair should be avoided if possible.)

- (Optional step) Brainstorm with different people who might help and pick one. (The teacher should encourage all possible helpers so the student can choose the best one.)

- Rehearse stating the problem, (the first step) and the question to be asked (accommodation to be requested).

- Make an appointment with the helper chosen and ask that person for assistance.

GRADE TRACKING

The purpose of the grade tracking strategy is to provide students with a way to record the grades they have earned. This strategy works especially well for students who have difficulty seeing the big picture. Students who tend to remember only the good news will find this helpful. The strategy requires students to record grades as they receive them and to use that information to determine which courses need the most attention.

- ◆ Steps
  - Give a record sheet, establish a grade goal for each class, and record that information.
  - At least once a day record grades received on a grade record sheet.
  - Calculate the current grade in each class at regular intervals. Daily calculation may be needed for some students while others may need to calculate their current averages weekly.
  - Use the liaison report or a teacher conference to confirm the accuracy of the student's information at regular intervals.
  - Compare the current grade average to the goals. Identify the subjects that are below the goal.
  - Form a plan of action to correct the mismatch between the grade and the goal.
  - Repeat the process.

SUBJECT:		
TERM:	GOAL:	
TEACHER:		
DATE	ASSIGNMENT	GRADE

SUBJECT:		
TERM:	GOAL:	
TEACHER:		
DATE	ASSIGNMENT	GRADE

Appendix I

Constructing for Knowledge

RAP

The purpose of the RAP strategy is to provide the students with a paraphrasing strategy designed to improve comprehension by focusing attention on important information and stimulating involvement with the materials. The strategy provides a framework for students to gain meaning from written information. The aim of the strategy is to teach students to engage in the internal dialogue necessary to think through an academic challenge. To gain the most benefit from this strategy, students must have previously been taught how to locate a main idea.

- ◆ Steps

    - **R**   read a paragraph or selection (silently or subvocally)

    - **A**   ask yourself "What are the main ideas or details of the paragraph?"

    - **P**   put the main idea into your own words with at least two details related to the main idea

Editing Partner Process

The purpose of the editing partner process is to instruct the student who has difficulty with the mechanics of writing in a strategy that will improve the quality of a composition. This strategy is also good for students whose written organization is weak. The strategy may need to be used after students have been taught a proofreading strategy such as COPS or POWER Writing.

- ◆ Steps

    - Take your rough draft to another person. (This can be an adult or another student—anyone who can suggest appropriate corrections.)

- Have someone read the composition aloud, word for word, while you listen. Consider:

  Does each sentence make sense?

  Does the composition as a whole make sense?

  Did I follow the assignment directions?

  Did I include all the points asked for in the assignment?

  Did I repeat the same word over and over?

  Have I left any thoughts or sentences incomplete?

  Are any of my sentences too long?

- When you hear an error, stop the reader and correct the error.
- Have an editor check for mechanical errors:

  spelling

  punctuation

  capitalization

  omissions

  verb tense

- Revise your paper neatly.

STEAL IT

The purpose of the steal it strategy is to teach the student a method of using the test instructions, directions, and previous questions to produce the best possible test answers, compositions, and topic sentences.

- ♦ Steps
  - Read the question or directions.
  - Use as many of the words and ideas from the directions and question as possible when composing your topic sentence or your thesis statement. Try turning the question into a statement and using that as your first sentence in a paragraph or essay.
  - Use previous test questions or directions to answer other questions.
  - Use grammar cues and clues to choose the best possible answer.

APPENDIX J

REPORTING PROGRESS AND ACCOMMODATIONS

TEACHER-STUDENT-PARENT COMMUNICATION MEMO

Student: _____ For the week ending: _____ FAX # _____

Student's Goals: _____

You have: (✔ indicates yes)	Phy. Science	Applied Math	Western Civ.	Learning Support	P. E.
Completed and handed in your assigned work on time					
Arrived on time with your materials					
Listened in class					
Expressed yourself appropriately					
Followed the class rules					
Used the class time to complete your assigned work					
Asked for help when needed					
Completed your assignment notebook accurately					
Worked toward achieving your goals					
Comments:					

Your work this week has been:	Phy. Science	Applied Math	Western Civ.	Learning Support	P. E.
Superior (A)					
Excellent (B)					
Average (C)					
Poor (D)					
Unacceptable (F)					

What you need to do next: (see assignment notebook for details)	Phy. Science	Applied Math	Western Civ.	Learning Support	P. E.
Homework:					
Test/Quiz preparation:					
Long-Term project:					
Essays:					
Other:					

STUDENT LIAISON REPORT

Student Name: _____ Grade Level: _____ Report Date: _____

Support Teacher: _____ Student Conference Date: _____ FAX #_____

This report has been compiled from a variety of sources, which might include one or more of the following: liaison reports from content teachers, cooperative planning sessions with teachers, direct inquiry of the content teacher, and the student. Information is collected once a cycle and may be as much as six school-days old before it is reported to the student and sent home to parents. The follow-through column will be filled during the student's next liaison conference.

Teacher	Subject	Student report	Teacher report	What I need to do next	Was I able to follow through?

Suggestions: _____

MONTHLY PLANNING LOG

Student _____ Grade Level _____ Month _____ 19___

Support Teacher _____ Student Conference Date _____

This report has been compiled from a variety of sources including one or more of the following: liaison reports from content teachers, cooperative sessions with teachers, direct inquiry of the content teacher, or student. Data is collected once a week and may be as much as five days old before it is recorded. This information is shared with the student once a month unless the information warrants a more immediate conference.

Teacher	Subject	Week #1 Date:	Week #2 Date:	Week #3 Date:	Week #4 Date:
Smith	English				
Santos	Health				
Chen	US Cult				
Woody	Music				
Student	J. Jones	Signature:	Signature:	Signature:	Signature:

Suggestions: _____

APPENDIX K

ORGANIZING TIME AND MATERIALS

MATERIALS CHECKLIST

The purpose of the materials checklist strategy is to provide the student with a systematic process for preparing to come to school, go to class, or leave school for home. The checklist should be customized for the individual student so that he or she can arrive at a task with all the necessary materials needed to complete the tasks he or she has been assigned.

- ◆ Steps

  - The student, with the guidance of the teacher, brainstorms all the materials needed for a typical day at school.

  - The student or teacher types up the list in the form of a checklist and places the checklist in a location that the student will readily see.

  - The student compares the checklist with the contents of his notebook or book bag before he leaves home for school and fills in any missing materials.

    and/or

  - The student prepares a checklist to use when leaving school for home. The steps are the same.

Student: _____

Do I have the following in my bookbag?

Two or more pencils	Folders for each subject
Eraser	My homework for each subject
Two or more pens	Spiral notebook for each subject
Notebook paper	Textbooks for each homework assignment
Phone # of my study partner	Assignment notebook

Assignment Tracking

The purpose of the assignment tracking strategy is to provide students with a way to record the assignments they have been given. This strategy works especially well for large tasks that seem overwhelming. Students who tend to put off tasks that cannot be done quickly will find this helpful. The strategy requires students to break assignments into small manageable pieces, to distinguish between completed work and work that still needs to be done at home, and to set a schedule for completing the work.

◆ Steps

- All daily assignments are recorded in an assignment notebook.

- Any assignments that are not completed by the end of the school day are highlighted.

- Any long-term assignments are broken into small subtasks. Then working back from the due date, students set a schedule for completing the work.

- As work progresses, the teacher should inquire about how well the students are keeping to the planned schedule.

- Teachers should also teach students how to replan, that is, how to change a schedule when tasks take more or less time than expected.

ASSIGNMENT NOTEBOOK GRADING SHEET

Student _____ Marking Period _____

Contents	Weekly grades							
1. School days noted month ahead								
2. Assignments recorded								
3. Grades recorded								
4. Long-term projects broken down								
5. Test preparation broken down								
TOTALS								

APPENDIX L

WHAT TO DO DURING THE TEST

TEST-TAKING ROUTINES

Test-taking routines are patterns of behavior that can be taught to students as standard steps to follow during a test. These routines guide students through a test, allowing them to apply their knowledge of the content quickly and accurately. Having a routine or pattern of behavior to follow during a test has the added benefit of relieving some of the anxiety and panic reactions that are common during tests.

These routines need to be taught to students in the same way other content skills need to be taught. They will require explanation and guided practice to become part of students' habitual behavior. Students need to learn the names of the steps and to be able to explain how they can apply them. Some students have developed their own routines through their personal test-taking experiences and will not need to learn a new routine. For other students, the steps in the routine will be a revelation.

TRIAGE

The purpose of the triage strategy is to teach the student a way to make efficient use of time during a test. This strategy works well for quizzes and more lengthy tests if a student can complete the entire test during a single class period. This strategy requires the student to divide the test into three parts (answers I know for sure, answers I can probably figure out, and answers I don't know) and to work from the known to the unknown.

- Read the entire test or quiz.

- During the first reading, identify the most difficult questions with an ✗, the middle difficult questions with a ?, and the easiest questions with a ★.

♦ Proceeding from the beginning of the test each time, answer all the ★ questions during the second reading, and the ? questions during the third trip through the test.

♦ The final reading will be to answer the ✗ questions. Because most of these answers will be guesses, very little of the test period should be devoted to these questions.

SPLASHDOWN

The splashdown technique is a memorization/rehearsal system that students can use during the test itself. As soon as students receive the test, information such as formulas, associations, and lists are written directly on the test and used for references during the test. The technique is described here because it must be consciously created during the rehearsal stage. The students must intend to use this method, identify what will be important to prepare as a splashdown, and practice writing the information before the test.

♦ Determine what information will be helpful as a guide during a test, (math formulas or steps, memory joggers and associations used, abbreviations, etc.) and write the information on notebook paper, index card, or Post-It.

♦ Practice writing the information quickly from short-term memory. This should take no more than one or two minutes.

♦ Take the written splashdown with you to the test. Refer to it until the instructor tells you to put it away.

♦ As soon as the test is handed out and before looking at the test questions, jot down as much of the splashdown as you remember.

♦ Use the information on your splashdown as a reference as you take the test. Include more information in minisplashdowns as they occur to you.

ELIMINATING OPTIONS

The purpose of teaching students to eliminate options is to provide a guide or a decision-making process for the identification of the distractors on a test. Students can find and cross-off the distractors, focus on the remaining options, and improve their chances of a correct response. This strategy can also be used with any assigned work that requires choosing among many options and is an essential skill for students who have a tendency to perseverate.

♦ Read the stem of the multiple choice question without looking at the options and try to answer the question. Read all the options and find the one that best matches the original response. If the student's answer is not an option given on the test, use the following guidelines to eliminate the options:

- If some of the answers are obviously wrong, cross them off

- If two answers are similar, except for one or two words, choose one of those

- If two quantities or dates are almost the same, choose one of those

- If two word choices sound similar (basalt, balsa), choose one of those

- If dates cover a wide range (1052, 1492, 1865), choose the one in the middle

♦ Use steal it—recognize and use names, dates, and places in other questions as clues to help answer more difficult questions.

♦ Read the stem with each option to see which answer best fits or sounds the most familiar.

♦ If all above strategies have failed, mark the question and leave it for later (sometimes the answer will "float" into working memory when ignored or another question will trigger the answer).

♦ If there is no penalty for guessing and you still cannot answer the question when you return to it, close your eyes, and pick an answer. You will be correct about 20 percent of the time.

REFERENCES

Adler, M. (1982). *The Paedia proposal*. New York: MacMillan.

Ausubel, D. B. (1968). *Educational psychology: A cognitive view*. New York: Holt, Rinehart & Winston.

Beech, M. (1988). *Pre-referral procedures*. [Brochure]. Florida Department of Education, Bureau of Education for Exceptional Students.

Bertrando, R., Conti-D'Antonio, M., & Eisenberger, J. (1992). *Unionville high school thinking skills: Final report*. Kennett Square, PA.

Beyer, B. K. (1991). *Teaching thinking skills: A handbook for secondary teachers*. Fairfax, VA: Allyn & Bacon.

Black, H., & Black, S. (1990). *Book II—organizing thinking: Graphic organizers*. Pacific Grove, CA: Midwest Publications.

Bloom, B. S. (1976). *Human characteristics and school learning*. New York: McGraw Hill.

Brooks, J. G., & Brooks, M. G. (1995). *In search of understanding: The case for constructivist classrooms*. Alexandria, VA: Association for Supervision and Curriculum Development.

Brophy, J. (1996). *Teaching problem students*. New York: Holt, Rinehart & Winston.

Canady, R. L., & Rettig, M. D. (1995). *Block scheduling: A catalyst for change in high schools*. Princeton, NJ: Eye On Education.

Canady, R. L., & Rettig, M. D. (1996). *Teaching in the block: Strategies for engaging active learners*. Princeton, NJ: Eye On Education.

Cawelti, G. (Ed.) (1995). *Handbook of research on improving student achievement*. Arlington, VA: Educational Research Service.

Cradler, J. (1986). Three messages regarding technology. *Social Studies Review, 25*, 8–29.

Costa, A. L. (1985). *Developing minds: A resource book for teaching thinking*. Alexandria, VA: Association for Supervision and Curriculum Development.

Costa, A. L. (1990). *The school as home for the mind*. Palatine, IL: Skylight Publishing.

Deschler, D. D., & Schumaker, J. B. (1984). Learning strategies: An instructional alternative for low achieving adolescents. *Exceptional Children, 52,* 583–590.

Ellis, E. S. (1995). *Watering-up the curriculum: Teaching for understanding.* Paper presented at the 11th Annual Learning Disorders Conference, Harvard University, Cambridge, MA.

Ellis, E. S. (1991). An instrumental model for teaching learning strategies. *Focus on Exceptional Children, 23,* 1–24.

Feuerstein, R. (1980). *Instrumental enrichment.* Baltimore: University Park Press.

Frank, A. R. (1973). Breaking down the learning tasks: A sequence approach. *Teaching Exceptional Children, 6,* 16–19.

Geocaris, C. (1996). Increasing student engagement: A mystery solved. *Education Leadership, 54,* 72–75.

Goldstein, A. P., Sparfkin, R. P., Geoshaw, J. N., & Klein, P. (1980). *Skill streaming the adolescent: A structured approach to teaching prosocial skills.* Champaign, IL: Research Press Company.

Goodman, Y. M. (1978). Kid-watching: An alternative to testing. *National Elementary School Principal, 57,* 41–45.

Hall, G. E., & Loucks, S. F. (1972). A developmental model for determining whether the treatment is actually implemented. *American Educational Research Journal, 14,* 236–276.

Herman, J. L., Aschbacher, P. R., & Winters, L. (1992). *A practical guide to alternative assessment.* Alexandria, VA: Association for Supervision and Curriculum Development.

Hyerle, D. (1996). *Visual tools.* Alexandria, VA: Association for Supervision and Curriculum Development.

Johnson, D. W., Johnson, R. T., Johnson-Holubec, E., & Roy, P. (1984). *Circles of learning, cooperation in the classroom.* Alexandria, VA: Association for Supervision and Curriculum Development.

Johnson, D. W. (1996). Assessing cooperative learning. *Education Update, 38,* 7.

Johnson, G. B., & Raven, P. H. (1996). *Biology: Principles and explorations.* New York: Holt, Rinehart & Winston, 28–30.

The Joint Committee on Teacher Planning for Students with Disabilities. (1995). *Planning for academic diversity in America's classrooms: Windows on reality, research, change, and practice.* Lawrence, KS: The University of Kansas Center for Research on Learning.

Kagen, S. (1988). *Cooperative learning: Resources for teachers.* Niguel, CA: Laguna Press.

Kounin, G. (1970). Discipline and group management in classrooms. In J. Brophy (Ed.). (1996). *Teaching problem students.* New York: Holt, Rinehart & Winston, 10–11.

Landfried, S. E. (1989). Enabling undermines responsibility in students. *Education Leadership, 47,* 61–65.

Margolis, H. (1990). Artful dimensions of collaborative consultation. In *Information edge: Language and language disorders.* Moorestown, NJ: Project Communication.

Marzano, R., & Arredondo, D. (1986). *Tactics for thinking.* Aurora, CO: Mid-Continent Regional Educational Laboratory.

McTighe, J. (1994). *A process for designing assessment tasks.* Baltimore, MD: Maryland Assessment Consortium.

Meltzer, L. J. (1992). *Strategy use in students with learning disabilities: The challenge of assessment, strategy assessment and instruction for students with learning disabilities: From theory to practice.* Austin, TX: Pro-Ed.

Meltzer, L.J. (Ed.). (1993). *Strategy assessment and instruction for students with learning disabilities—from theory to practice.* Austin, TX: Pro-Ed.

Miles, D. D., & Forcht, J. P. (1995). Mathematical strategies for secondary students with learning disabilities or mathematics deficiencies: A cognitive approach. *Intervention in School and Clinic, 31,* 91–96.

Miller, S. P. , & Mercer, C. D. (1993). Mnemonics: Enhancing the math performance of students with learning difficulties. In L. J. Meltzer, D. P. Haynes, K. Rafter Biddle, M. Paster, & S. E.Taber (Eds), *Strategies for success—interventions in school and clinic* (pp. 84–95). Austin, TX: Pro-Ed.

Olsen, D. G. (1995). "Less" can be "more" in the promotion of thinking. *Social Education, 59,* 130–134.

Palincsar, A. S., & Brown, A. L. (1994). Reciprocal teaching of comprehension—fostering and monitoring activities. *Cognition and Instruction, 1,* 111–175.

Polloway, E. (1996). Treatment acceptability: Determining appropriate intervention within inclusive classrooms. *Intervention in School and Clinic, 31,* 133–144.

Perrone, V. (1994). How to engage students in learning. *Educational Leadership, 51,* 11–13.

Reid, K. D. (1993). Learning disorders and the flavors of cognitive science. *Education Leadership, 54,* 18–22.

Rimm, S. (1997). An underachievement epidemic. *Education Leadership, 54,* 19–22.

Roy, P. A. (1990). *Students learning together.* Richfield, MN: Patricia Roy Company.

Salend, S. J. (1995). Modifying tests for diverse learners. *Intervention in School and Clinic, 11,* 84–90.

Saphier, J., & Haley, M. A. (1993). *Summarizers—activity structures to support integration and retention of new learning.* Carlise, MA: Research for Better Teaching.

Schon, D. (1987). *Educating the reflective practitioner.* San Francisco: Jossey-Bass.

Simon, C. (1987). *Classroom communication screening procedure for early adolescents.* Tempe, AZ: CommuniCog Publications.

Slavin, R. E. (1986). Are cooperative learning and untracking harmful to the gifted? *Educational Leadership, 48,* 60.

Sternberg, R. J. (1997). What does it mean to be smart? *Educational Leadership, 54,* 20–24.

Thomas, A., & Grimes, J. (1985). *Best practices in school-based consultation.* Kent, OH: National Association of School Psychologists.

Vaughn, S., & Thousand, J. S. (1995). Responsible inclusion for students with learning disabilities. *Journal of Learning Disabilities, 28,* 264–270.

Udvari-Solner, A., & Thousand, J. S. (1995). Promising practices that foster inclusive education. In R. A. Villa & J. S. Thousand (Eds.), *Creating an inclusive school* (pp. 110–124). Alexandria, VA: Association for Supervision and Curriculum Development.

Wiggins, G. (1993). Standards, not standardization. *Educational Leadership, 48,* 18–25.